The Series on Social E~

Teachers
in partnership with the Center fo
and the Collaborative to Advance So

Jonathan Cohen

Making Your School Safe:
Strategies to Protect Children and Promote Learning
John Devine and Jonathan Cohen

School–Family Partnerships for Children's Success
Evanthia N. Patrikakou, Roger P. Weissberg,
Sam Redding, and Herbert J. Walberg, editors

Building Academic Success on Social and Emotional Learning:
What Does the Research Say?
Joseph E. Zins, Roger P. Weissberg,
Margaret C. Wang, and Herbert J. Walberg, editors

How Social and Emotional Development Add Up:
Getting Results in Math and Science Education
Norris M. Haynes, Michael Ben-Avie,
and Jacque Ensign, editors

Higher Expectations: Promoting Social Emotional Learning
and Academic Achievement in Your School
Raymond J. Pasi

Caring Classrooms/Intelligent Schools:
The Social Emotional Education of Young Children
Jonathan Cohen, editor

Educating Minds and Hearts:
Social Emotional Learning and the Passage into Adolescence
Jonathan Cohen, editor

Social emotional learning is now recognized as an essential aspect of children's education and a necessary feature of all successful school reform efforts. The books in this series will present perspectives and exemplary programs that foster social and emotional learning for children and adolescents in our schools, including interdisciplinary, developmental, curricular, and instructional contributions. The three levels of service that constitute social emotional learning programs will be critically presented: (1) curriculum-based programs directed to all children to enhance social and emotional competencies, (2) programs and perspectives intended for special needs children, and (3) programs and perspectives that seek to promote the social and emotional awareness and skills of educators and other school personnel.

Making Your School Safe

STRATEGIES TO PROTECT CHILDREN AND PROMOTE LEARNING

John Devine and Jonathan Cohen

Foreword by Maurice J. Elias

Teachers College, Columbia University
New York and London

Published by Teachers College Press, 1234 Amsterdam Avenue, New York, NY 10027

Library of Congress Cataloging-in-Publication Data

Devine, John.
   Making your school safe : strategies to protect children and promote learning / John Devine & Jonathan Cohen.
        p. cm.—(Series on social emotional learning)
     Includes bibliographical references and index.
     ISBN 978-0-8077-4783-4 (pbk. : alk. paper)—ISBN 978-0-8077-4784-1 (cloth : alk. paper)
     1. Schools—United States—Safety measures. 2. School violence—United States—Prevention. 3. School crisis management—United States. I. Cohen, Jonathan, 1952- II. Title.
   LB2866.D48 2007
   363.11'371—dc22   2006038067

ISBN: 978-0-8077-4783-4 (paper)
ISBN: 978-0-8077-4784-1 (cloth)

Printed on acid-free paper
Manufactured in the United States of America

14   13   12   11   10   09   08   07   8   7   6   5   4   3   2   1

To Betty, who is the other half of my soul. (JD)

To Stacey, who helps to provide a foundation for safety and connectedness that supports all of my learning and work. (JC)

Contents

Foreword

Among the many books you will read about school safety, this one will make you think, feel, and act in ways that are likely to improve the conditions of the school you are in. Why will this happen? In part, it will be the compelling content, presented in clear and easy to follow formats. You will learn about formulating crisis plans, safety plans, ways to promote students' social-emotional competencies, addressing bullying in systematic, ecologically comprehensive ways, and working with traumatized children in an effective and dignified manner. You will also learn about models for promoting learning in the context of a safe school.

However, as valuable as this guidance may sound, it is the way the information is presented that is distinctive and provides potency to its influence. This book is built on a socially and emotionally informed pedagogy: Chapters begin with vignettes and end with a set of reflective questions.

The approach taken by the authors deeply respects the wisdom and experience of adult learners. There is no pretense that readers have somehow not heard much if not most of the information presented here. The names—Olweus, Comer, Berkowitz, the Collaborative for Academic, Social, and Emotional Learning, Selman, Guerra, Twemlow, Watson, Greenberg—are leaders of the fields of school safety, bully and violence prevention, social-emotional learning, and caring learning communities. Their work, as well as the work of the Center for Social and Emotional Education, is drawn upon skillfully. Yet, we all know well the limit of information alone without emotional engagement.

The vignettes are meant to activate readers' emotions by fostering recollections of experiences similar to those portrayed by the vignettes. Doing so creates a deeper level of connection to the material that each chapter contains. But there is more. The reflective questions that conclude each chapter are, to me, the keys to action. For as we ask ourselves these simple questions, we are forced to confront the challenges that many of these questions contain. What is the essence of these challenges? It is this: Are we doing all we should, and all that children deserve, and all that is within our capability, to protect children and promote learning?

Below are some of the questions that the material in this book will help you answer better, including finding actions to foster high-quality implementation of needed interventions:

- Do you (as a principal, teacher, other staff member, parent) feel physically, socially, and emotionally safe in your school?
- Do you have a team approach to safety and an ongoing process for crisis preparedness? What does your school crisis plan delineate? What are the most important details? How many people in your school know about the existence of the plan? How many people really know what to do?
- Do students tell adults when they feel unsafe in school?
- Do teachers believe that an important part of their job is to teach social and emotional skills, knowledge, and beliefs?
- What do you do now as an educator to foster students' emotional safety in your class? To foster students' emotional safety in school?
- To what extent is there a school-wide commitment to not tolerating bullying and to the notion that we must all actively stand up to bully–victim behavior, as opposed to inadvertently falling into a passive bystander role?
- As you reflect on students that you suspect or know have been traumatized, do you consider the signs of possible trauma.
- Who in particular has contributed to the success of initiatives designed to promote learning and to protect children? What are the attributes of their contribution?

What can we learn? Do we take time to celebrate what is working? Who owns this initiative? How might we continue to expand the ownership of this effort?

As educators dedicated to the well-being of children and to their learning, once we ask ourselves these challenging questions, we cannot rest until we find satisfactory answers. This book will help you keep the challenges in the forefront and aid you in your essential quest for answers.

—Maurice J. Elias, Ph.D., Rutgers University
Director, Rutgers Social-Emotional Learning Lab
Founding Member, Leadership Team, CASEL
(Collaborative for Academic, Social, and Emotional Learning)

Acknowledgments

We are very grateful to our colleagues at the Center for Social and Emotional Education as well as CSEE's Board of Trustees who supported this work in so many ways. We are also indebted to David Schonfeld and Roy Lubit whose expertise has enriched this work.

Introduction

People need to feel safe, socially and emotionally as well as physically. Think about a moment in your life when you did not feel safe. It is easy to see how feeling unsafe emotionally complicates—indeed precludes—our ability to listen, reflect, think clearly, and learn. There has been a growing awareness over the last two decades that physical and social violence are shockingly common in our K–12 schools. More and more states and school districts have developed policies and programs that address violence and safety. To a great extent, these efforts have focused almost exclusively on physical violence. Yet, physical violence and social emotional violence in schools are intertwined. In recent years, physical violence has been on the decline. However, social emotional violence has not. It is ubiquitous and undermines children's and adolescents' ability to learn and develop in healthy ways.

This book is designed to serve as a tool to help schools review and further develop their school safety plans. We have synthesized research and best practices from the fields of character education, social emotional learning, risk prevention, and physical and mental health. There are many excellent school safety handbooks on the market; this book is not one of them. We are not dealing only with physical safety here but with the intersection of physical safety with social, emotional, and ethical education and their combined consequent impact on the academic life of the school.

A growing body of research shows how effectively social, emotional, ethical, and academic education promote the competency of the individual child and can at the same time ensure safer, more caring, more participatory, and more responsive schools (Bar-On et al., 2007; Cohen, 2006). A number of research reports, including the American Psychological Association's (2003) Presidential Task Force report, have concluded that we now have the knowledge and the practical guidelines to translate these research findings into school improvement guidelines, educational practices, and policies (Cohen, 2001; Elias et al., 2006; Weissberg, Kumpfer, & Seligman, 2003; Zins, Weissberg, Walberg, & Wang, 2003). In other words, we now have a great deal of know-how about what steps to take to promote social and emotional as well as physical safety in our schools. In this book, we describe many interventions culled from research and practice literature about what steps contribute to effective social, emotional, and ethical education—and therefore to school safety and academic excellence.

A number of studies now confirm the intuitively correct conclusion that social emotional education enhances both academic performance and school safety. Our Center for Social and Emotional Education's research database on social emotional and character education lists empirical studies in this area (www.csee.net).

Social, emotional, ethical, and academic education refers to the process of teaching students to "read" themselves and others in order to solve social, emotional, and ethical problems and to become ongoing social, emotional, and ethical learners. Just as physical education builds a child's muscles and motor skills, social, emotional, ethical, and academic education builds a child's self-reflective and empathic capabilities. Children learn to control impulses, communicate sensitive issues more clearly, cooperate, become more self-motivating, learn how to become a friend, and become more altruistic.

Research shows that there are two core processes that promote children's abilities in these areas. The first occurs when teachers in the classroom actively teach children to be more socially and emotionally competent and ethically inclined. The second occurs within the context of the total school when adults work systemically and cooperatively to create safer, more caring, and more responsive schools.

Social, emotional, ethical, and academic education means much more than just learning politeness and good manners. It also means that both staff members and students should strive for ethical behavior and to become responsible citizens living in a democracy, conscious of the human rights and needs of others within the global community. In other words, children learn how to reflect and empathize and use this information to solve problems in creative and flexible ways.

We adults are always social, emotional, and ethical teachers whenever we work with a child in school or when we parent at home. We adults are always teaching, whether we like it or not, whether we are conscious of it or not. It is well known that how adults act is often much more powerful than what they say. Some of the key questions to consider are:

- What are the social, emotional, and ethical lessons we want children to learn?
- Are we purposefully and helpfully teaching children the skills and dispositions that will support them to be reflective and responsible members of a democracy?
- Are we actively inculcating the emotional and ethical lessons that help children to solve problems nonviolently and to develop in healthy ways?

Most parents, when choosing a school for their children, have something even more fundamental in mind than academics: safety. Most parents consider safety their top priority. They will check out a school carefully before enrolling their child to make sure that it is the kind of place in which their child will feel safe—and be safe—socially and emotionally as well as physically. Parents chat with other parents about their impressions about the school before enrolling their child. We have known inner-city parents who check with a friendly school security guard about the school's reputation. Unfortunately, many inner-city parents do not have the luxury of obtaining a safe school for their children.

ORGANIZATION OF THIS BOOK

Each of the chapters in this book opens with one or more vignettes based on our experience in working with children and schools.

We draw on these vignettes as we discuss the main points of the chapter. Then each chapter closes with a list of questions to help you reflect on your current practices related to the topic of the chapter.

Chapter 1 raises and attempts to answer the basic and most obvious question about our topic: Why this sudden interest in the relationship between social emotional education and safety? Why now, at this point in the history of American education? In Chapter 1, we attempt to answer this question by analyzing two vignettes that illustrate two of the principal educational phenomena of the past 2 decades: the spate of school violence incidents and the appearance of the No Child Left Behind law.

Chapter 2 presents, in outline form, the essentials of a crisis response plan and stresses the importance of the school leadership being convinced that the planning process must be built into the fiber of the school's life. We might summarize Chapter 2 with that saying often seen in literature on fire departments: "Safety is no accident." School safety plans must be living documents. They must be constantly rehearsed dramas whose script all the actors know by heart.

In Chapter 3, we delineate how feeling safe socially and emotionally provides the optimal foundation for learning and healthy development. Whether we feel safe or not influences our emotional experiences, which in turn influence our social experiences. In this chapter, the focus is on a series of steps that adults and students alike can take to create a climate of learning and safety in school, which serves as a primary violence prevention intervention and promotes healthy youth development.

Chapter 4 focuses on the second core dimension of social and emotional safety which enhances the likelihood that children and adults will feel safe in schools: direct classroom teaching and learning that enhances social and emotional competencies.

Chapter 5 builds on the discussions of the two previous chapters, namely, the insight that the social and emotional aspects of safety are usually interactive. If there is no sense of safety in the school as a totality, it does little good if an individual teacher attempts to hold the fort single-handedly in her or his classroom. In this chapter, we focus on students' sense of emotional safety and the steps we can take to promote this foundational dimension of feeling safe in schools.

In Chapter 6, we come face-to-face with the reverse side of social emotional education. What happens when social and emotional learning breaks down? We consider this outcome in the context of the issue of bullying. When an incident of bullying occurs, the very ideal of a school as a place of learning is ruptured. European researchers have been studying the phenomenon of bullying since the early 1970s, but in recent years U.S. scholars have been contributing their own insights. In this chapter, we study the impact of bullying on the individual and on the school, as well as some of the more successful schoolwide prevention methods for eradicating it.

Chapter 7 deals with an often underrecognized problem— childhood trauma. We can all recall highly publicized cases in recent years in which emotional trauma from physical or emotional abuse affected a child, even to the point of causing the child's death. This chapter deals with the safety issues relating to childhood trauma, including the ways in which learning is affected. Recognizing and knowing how to refer traumatized children for treatment will simultaneously help the individual and improve the atmosphere of the entire school.

In Chapter 8, our closing chapter, we suggest a model of school improvement that integrates research from a number of fields: risk prevention, K–12 education, health promotion, social emotional learning, and character education. This process of social, emotional, ethical, and academic school improvement brings the community together to understand the current strengths and challenges that are inadvertently undermining school safety in order to promote learning and the healthy development of K–12 students.

This book is written for the full range of schools: elementary, middle, and secondary. Although school violence incidents in high school have been highly publicized, clearly effective violence prevention efforts must be made at all levels from kindergarten to 12th grade. In fact, feeling unsafe—socially, emotionally, and often physically—typically begins in the elementary school years. When all schools integrate the instructional and systemic dimensions described in the following chapters, they are not only preventing problems but also promoting the social, emotional, ethical, and academic skills and dispositions that provide the foundation for lifelong learning and the capacity to love, work, and participate in a democracy.

CHAPTER ONE

The Relationship Between Social Emotional Education and Safety in a School

> During fourth period, Sue came over and sat with me in a corner of the cafeteria. She brought her biology book and studied a bit, and then decided just to sit and talk. She started telling me about the gangs in the school. She said that most of her friends tried to stay away from them. Sometimes it was hard because the gang members always harassed her. She said that it was hard to ignore them, so she ended up just keeping to herself or spending her lunch with me. I told her that it was for the best.

> Peter, one of the friendliest of the middle school students, came running over to see me this morning. He said that he was so excited because he had just heard that the school was going to get a metal detector system installed. He said that he knew he was going to feel safer from now on because there would not be so many weapons in the school. I have to admit I was a bit perplexed as to how I, a teacher, should respond to him. At the same time, one of the school safety agents told me that some students give them a bad time just to show their fellow students that they are tough guys, not to be messed with. This seems to be a creative approach to dealing with harassment and bullying on the part of some students, but what does it say about the school climate?

Feeling safe in school—socially and emotionally as well as physically—shapes student learning and development. We all need to feel safe to discover, learn, and relate in healthy ways. Students and school personnel, for example, all appreciate that a fire is dangerous. It is well known that we need to help all members of the school community understand how dangerous a fire can be and provide opportunities to practice what to do in such an emergency. The underlying thesis of this book is that the same holds true for social and emotional dangers. We all tend to deny them to a greater or lesser extent—life and learning can be anxiety provoking and scary. Whether a student is facing a bully or just the prospect of raising a hand to ask a question, it is normal to feel anxiety and fear. Over the last several decades, there has been a growing awareness that feeling socially and emotionally unsafe powerfully complicates and undermines positive youth development and student learning. How can we help students and school staff alike appreciate that we need to understand the range of social emotional dangers and consider helpful (and unhelpful) ways of coping with these dangers? This volume focuses on the range of physical, social, and emotional factors involved in feeling safe at school. Our goal is to translate research and best practices into guidelines that will assist you as you go about making your school safe.

Two underlying frameworks provide the foundation for this book. First, to make schools truly safe, we always need to consider three overlapping levels of school life: the school as a whole, the classroom, and the individual. School leaders define an ethos for the entire school. They set the goals, the norms, and the spirit of how all the actors on the school scene treat one another. Thinking systemically allows school leaders to foster a climate for learning and safety. However, it is inside the classroom that students learn specific skills, knowledge, and dispositions. Ultimately, teaching and learning occurs on a child-by-child basis. We need to understand what the learning and safety-related needs of all students are. For example, many students who bully at school are being victimized at home or in their neighborhoods. To make our schools safe, we need to understand how individual student issues such as this are shaping relationships and the climate of our class-rooms, hallways, and school as a whole.

The second framework is social, emotional, ethical, and academic education. Educators and other adult members of the school community are always social, emotional, and ethical teachers. What varies is how conscious the adults are about the lessons that they are teaching and how helpful these lessons are. In fact, a growing body of research suggests that evidence-based social, emotional, ethical, and academic learning initiatives provide the optimal foundation for violence prevention efforts in K–12 schools (American Psychological Association, 2003; Catalano, Berglund, Ryan, Lonczak, & Hawkins, 2002; Zins et al., 2003). Over the last 3 decades, a growing body of research from K–12 education, char-acter education, social emotional learning, risk prevention, and physical and mental health promotion has shown that there are two essential processes that reduce violence and promote student learning: (1) promoting K–12 students' social, emotional, and cog-nitive competencies and ethical dispositions; and (2) working to create a safe, caring, participatory, and responsive school. We use the terms *social emotional learning*, *character education*, and *social, emotional, ethical, and academic education* interchangeably. Histori-cally, there were very significant differences between character education and social emotional learning, but evidence-based work in these areas is now much more similar than different (see Co-hen, 2006, for a detailed discussion of this development).

As schools refine their safety plans, they may wish to consider how emotional issues—like recognizing each person's contribu-tion to the task at hand, respect, cooperation, and teamwork—permeate even the most basic material and physical part of the plan, the facilities, the fire and multihazard drills, the incident command system, and communications with police, fire, and emergency medical services. All school safety planning rests on an assurance that the school is physically safe. Clearly, this foun-dation of physical safety—preparation for fires, gun incidents, and even terrorist calamities—is absolutely essential for a truly comprehensive school safety plan. But in and of itself, limiting the plan to the material, physical level alone is not enough.

THE IMPORTANCE OF SOCIAL AND EMOTIONAL SAFETY

The question naturally arises: *Why has social and emotional safety become so important now?* Going back to our foundational thesis, if social and emotional learning is the bedrock on which school safety rests, and if school safety is the cornerstone on which the whole academic structure rests, then it is clear that social and emotional learning is vital. Why is this truth (which is also the basic assumption underlying all genuine school reform and restructuring) just now emerging into the light of our communal consciousness? We believe that at least two factors account for the growing prominence of social emotional learning and character education (SEL/CE) at present. The first is the school violence phenomenon. There was a time when schools were presumed to be safe havens and no one gave much thought to school security. The school was considered to be a kind of sanctuary. Then suddenly there emerged on the national scene a series of school tragedies culminating in the so-called spree shootings at Columbine High School and elsewhere during the late 1990s. Within the school violence prevention movement, our country's overdependence on technology (in the form of metal detectors, etc.) became apparent and educators began looking for more substantive solutions to help students be more secure in schools. It became clear that SEL/CE encompasses a whole range of initiatives that are the polar opposite of the technosecurity approach.

The second factor accounting for the rise of SEL/CE has been the overemphasis on standardized exams, test preparation, and academic achievement. With the almost exclusive concentration on the teacher as instructor and "teaching to the test" in recent decades, and especially since the enactment of the No Child Left Behind law, the role of the teacher as a caring parental figure—in loco parentis—had become almost completely forgotten. As a union official in a large urban school district told one of us, "In loco parentis? That's history!" But the tide is now turning in the other direction. More and more historical and contemporary evidence is accumulating that, paradoxically, the most academically successful schools have been the very ones that have insisted on the importance of social and emotional safety.

Note the importance of what happens as the social-emotional-safety side of the school agenda upends and deconstructs the academic side. Our very conception of the notion of school as an institution becomes redefined. We begin to think of a school not primarily as a place where instruction takes place and where tests are given but as a community whose members (teachers, students, other staff) form a group with common characteristics, common interests, mutual respect, and shared ethical ideals.

Paradoxically, schools that have given priority to emotional safety and to social and emotional growth in their students have also been recognized as the most successful ones academically. It is clear, then, that academic excellence follows the successful infusion of SEL/CE into a school. SEL/CE is the basis for school safety (physical, social, and emotional) without which concentration on serious study and learning cannot take place. We are far from implying that SEL/CE is more important than the academic side of school life. We are saying that inculcating social and emotional skills both within classrooms and within the whole school context is the surest way to attain both academic excellence and social and emotional safety.

CONSIDERING THE CASES

One place to begin to reflect on the positive impact of SEL/CE on physical, social, and emotional safety is examples of incidents in schools that are deficient in inculcating SEL/CE. Both scenarios at the beginning of this chapter are opportunities to profitably meditate on how to deal with the issues raised. The questions below are suggestions only, for your solitary reflection or to stimulate a discussion among colleagues. There are no right answers to most of these questions, and the answers will always depend on the local conditions in each school and community.

Reflecting on Sue's Dilemma

In light of the initial discussion on the significance of social emotional education, what are your thoughts on rereading the anecdote about Sue, the girl who came over and sat with a teacher in the corner of the cafeteria? Perhaps the first point to make is the fact that the teacher is available for Sue in the cafeteria. This raises a basic question: How available are staff members in your school for informal conversations with students? It may be that the gang problem is so serious that it is beyond the control of the school. Perhaps it is a matter for the police. But whether Sue is being harassed by a gang or just by a clique of other girls, she is seeking out an adult relationship in the hope of resolving this peer-related problem. Sue will not feel emotionally, socially, or perhaps even physically safe in the school until this issue is resolved. Perhaps she sees the teacher as a role model whose behavior and demeanor she hopes to imitate. In recent years, teachers' unions have sought to have cafeteria duty removed from the list of a teacher's tasks, and this responsibility has been turned over to school safety agents. Yet informal cafeteria and playground duties can be ideal occasions for adults to socialize with students and relate to them on a personal basis. It is sometimes said that in American culture we adults have washed our hands of the dirty job of adolescent initiation rites. Sue and her mentor, sitting and talking quietly in a corner of the cafeteria, are a good example of how an adult can reimmerse herself in the sometimes messy job of adolescent development. How do you feel about teachers and educators taking on the role of *in loco parentis*?

Analyzing Peter's Naive Assumption

Peter's assumption—that his school was going to become safer after the introduction of metal detectors—may sound naive, but some students in highly troubled schools have indeed had such hopes. But relying on techno-security devices alone has proven to be a false hope time and again. There is no doubt that metal detectors, screening devices, and other high-tech aids are needed in some neighborhoods, especially given that our society permits the proliferation of weapons. But as the second part of the vignette makes clear, if teachers and school staff do not convey a sense of social and emotional ownership in the school, then students feel that they are on their own when it comes to control of the corridors and the public space of the building. Youths feel that adults have abandoned them to their own devices, and so every student must watch his or her back when it come to dealing with gangs, cliques, and antisocial elements in the school. When this happens, students report that they have to present themselves as being tough. Then a sense of trust disappears and the school climate prevents healthy social emotional and academic learning.

In the chapters that follow, we make suggestions regarding bullying, cliques, and gangs that you may wish to incorporate into your own toolkit. In this chapter, we hope that we have begun to make clear that there is a strong relationship among (1) physical, emotional, and social safety; (2) social emotional learning; and (3) the placid atmosphere that is required for the academic side of school life to thrive.

SUMMARY

Feeling safe is a basic need for students, educators, and other school personnel. Most schools focus on physical safety alone and overlook how social emotional safety provides an essential foundation for learning and positive youth development. Comprehensive and effective K–12 school safety programs need to be grounded in three overlapping levels:

- Individual—recognizing, addressing, and anticipating the needs of out-of-control and at-risk students
- Classroom—teaching students the social, emotional,

and ethical as well as cognitive skills and dispositions
that support nonviolent conflict resolution, flexible
problem solving, and learning
- Schoolwide—adults and students working to create a
  climate for learning and safety

Evidence-based social, emotional, ethical, and academic learning initiatives provide the optimal foundation for violence prevention efforts in K–12 schools. These efforts need to be grounded in
two overlapping processes: (1) promoting K–12 students' social,
emotional, and cognitive competencies and ethical dispositions;
and (2) working to create safe, caring, participatory, and responsive schools.

REFLECTING ON YOUR CURRENT PRACTICE

- Do you (as a principal, teacher, other staff member,
  parent) feel physically, socially, and emotionally safe
  in your school?
- Is the learning environment such that it promotes academic exploration and an atmosphere for thoughtful
  reflection, scholarly discourse, and study?
- Do staff members uniformly attempt to instill social
  and emotional learning and inculcate respect?
- Is there a conscious effort to teach respect and link it
  to safety? For example, do the school safety officers address students with respect?
- Do staff members treat one another with respect and
  courtesy, thereby setting an example for students?
- Do teachers, as a group and as individuals, attempt to
  inculcate social and emotional skills in the corridors
  and stairwells and the cafeteria, as well as in their
  classrooms?
- What SEL/CE practices are you engaging in already in
  your school that might serve as models for other schools?
- Are SEL/CE, safety, and academic learning intertwined in your school? How?

CHAPTER TWO

Preparing Your School to Deal with a Crisis: Principles of School Crisis Preparedness and Response

with David Schonfeld

The principal of a middle school receives a phone call from the police on Friday morning informing her that one of the students was fatally shot earlier that morning. Shortly thereafter, a teacher contacts the office to report that he overheard a couple of students commenting that the student was killed by a rival gang and there were concerns about retaliation during a scheduled school dance that evening. The principal convenes an emergency meeting of the school crisis team to address the following issues: (1) How will the school verify the information about the student's death? (2) How should the school handle the alleged threats of gang retaliation and what steps should the school take to decrease the risk of further violence? (3) What information should be provided to students, staff, and parents, and when should this occur; how should the school handle anticipated media inquiries? (4) What supports should be put in place to help students and staff cope with the death of a member of the school community? (5) What changes in the school schedule might be appropriate? Other issues are raised and addressed in the meeting.

Chapter 1 stressed the importance of social and emotional learning as the basis of both safety and instruction. In most school systems, the group delegated to review and revise the school safety plan is the school safety committee. In the wake of tragic events over the course of the past 15 years, many schools have set up school crisis teams to respond to the unique circumstances that surround any crisis. This chapter outlines the basic principles recommended by school safety experts for instituting a crisis preparedness planning process and spells out the roles and responsibilities of school crisis team members.

Experts agree that undergoing a crisis preparedness planning process and instituting prevention efforts that deal with school safety and security, as well as those that address the personal and emotional needs of the students, can go a long way toward reducing the likelihood that a crisis will occur (Schonfeld, Lichtenstein, Kline-Pruett, & Speese-Linehan, 2002). Nevertheless, crises can and will happen; our job is to reduce the negative impacts when they do occur. As the opening vignette illustrates, crisis situations confront schools with the need to make many pressing and critical decisions that will impact the physical safety and emotional well-being of students and staff. In the absence of prior planning and preparation, many schools may find themselves overwhelmed with the task of responding to these needs with limited relevant expertise, insufficient time, and limited resources. Those schools that have devoted the necessary time and energy to crisis preparedness planning, developing procedures and policies, and establishing a functioning school crisis team are often surprised that an otherwise overwhelming crisis can become instead a difficult, but manageable, event.

INSTITUTING A CRISIS PREPAREDNESS PROCESS

Many, if not all, schools today have a standard crisis response plan that has been adopted at the school district level. It is nevertheless crucial that each school adapt that plan to be fully responsive to the unique needs of the community and the individual school. Plans that exist only on paper are clearly useless. It is crucial that the planning process be built into the fiber of the school's life.

Some school jurisdictions provide only a skeletal model that, in some cases, is little more than a checklist of procedures and caveats. But crisis planning is more than just a one-shot stab at putting together a crisis plan. Schools need to be convinced that building the planning process has to become an integral part of the ongoing pedagogy. Many manuals and workbooks exist to flesh out the security framework. Each school needs to evaluate the available models and decide which one fits best. Several models exist in both book and online form, and we present one such model in Chapter 8.

The clearest, simplest, and most readable approach to crisis response is *How to Prepare for and Respond to a Crisis*, by David Schonfeld and associates (Schonfeld et al., 2002). This handbook draws on over a decade of experience of the School Crisis Prevention and Response Initiative of the National Center for Children Exposed to Violence (www.nccev.org), which was established in 1991 as a collaboration of the Yale Child Study Center and community mental health professionals, law enforcement representatives, and local and state educational agencies. Schonfeld and colleagues developed an organizational model for school crisis preparedness and response to help schools develop the internal capacity to address the safety and mental health needs of children and staff in times of crisis (Schonfeld, Kline, & Members of the Crisis Intervention Committee, 1994). The program subsequently provided training to tens of thousands of school-related staff throughout the country and abroad, as well as technical assistance during hundreds of school crisis events. After September 11, 2001, the School Crisis Response Initiative began working with the New York City public schools to help optimize the infrastructure within the school system for crisis preparedness and response. The group provided training for school crisis teams in all 1,200 schools serving 1.1 million students so that each school would have a working school crisis response team that is part of an integrated, citywide response network.

The main reason we recommend this group's approach to crisis response is that it incorporates into crisis planning the importance of fostering social and emotional competencies as a sound basis for school security and safety. The following key concepts define the foundation on which the School Crisis Response Initiative bases its approach to crisis response:

- In times of crisis, students, their families, and school staff will find most support from those they already know and trust. The best response to a crisis, even if it is related to a national or international event, is a local response. School personnel know the students, their families, the local community, and the local culture well and can tailor the school's response in a way that outside experts cannot. Since children's responses to a crisis can continue for months or even years, a school-based team is best suited to provide ongoing monitoring and service. Outside experts can serve a vital role in providing consultation, technical assistance, and support to school staff, but most direct services are optimally provided by local personnel. An effective school crisis team and school crisis response sends a powerful message to the community that the school is prepared to deal with even the most challenging events that confront schoolchildren and their families. Isn't that what all parents want to believe about their children's school?
- Schools cannot effectively plan how to respond to a crisis while a crisis is occurring. Prior preparation and planning are critical. Schools should develop general protocols and procedures for responding to a crisis, establish school crisis teams with designated roles and responsibilities, and participate in ongoing training and professional development so that school crisis plans are working documents (and not simply unread documents that clutter bookshelves) and school crisis teams are well-functioning teams. The issue is not whether a crisis will occur, but rather what it will entail and, most important, what the school system is prepared to do to minimize the impact on students and staff.
- To help guide the work of the school crisis team, it is important to have an organizational model that delin-

eates the roles and responsibilities of team members at both the district and school levels and outlines procedures and protocols for both generic and specific crisis events. These plans and procedures should be standardized throughout the school district (with oversight by a district-level team), but specifics should be modified so that the plan is responsive to the unique needs and vulnerabilities of each school.

- The response should address the physical safety, emotional well-being, and information needs of the students, staff, parents, and, when appropriate, the general community. As illustrated in the opening vignette, it is impossible to address any one of these needs without addressing the other two. Many schools have separate teams or individuals that address each of these three areas—a school safety team, a mental health team, and a public information office—and then expect that an administrator who may not even be part of each group can somehow coordinate and integrate the response of the three separate groups during a crisis. A coordinated school crisis response plan anticipates that these issues are interconnected and ensures that the appropriate staff are all part of the same response team.

- While concerns about terrorism such as the events of 9/11 have highlighted the fact that major crisis events are possible, the crisis response plan should not be applicable only to large-scale events. School systems are often confronted with more common crisis events, such as the death of a student or staff member by accidental causes or illness, which nonetheless have a major impact on the school community, and can benefit from a coordinated and thoughtful crisis response. Experience in planning for and responding to such events will help ensure that the crisis response plans are feasible and the school crisis team is a well-functioning and experienced team. If the team is able to respond to a crisis such as the one in the opening vignette, they will be in a much better position to address a potential terrorist attack. Events that characteristically benefit from a crisis team approach include death of a student or staff member, natural disasters, accidents or other threats to the safety or health of students and staff, and threats to the emotional well-being of the school community.

- School crisis response plans should not be developed or implemented by schools in isolation. It is important to reach out to members of the local and regional community to identify groups and individuals to collaborate in the development of plans and the provision of services in the event of a crisis. Members of the community can and should serve on the school crisis team. It is important, though, to identify these groups and individuals prior to any crisis event and form the relationships that allow them to become part of the extended school community so that they can be called upon during a crisis. Schools can serve as the site of a community-wide response to a crisis event, drawing upon resources and expertise within the broader community to support students and staff, and thereby also increasing parent and community-wide ties to their local schools.

- Any crisis that impacts the students will generally impact the school staff as well, including the members of the school crisis team. School staff are better able to support their students if they themselves are receiving support. Any school crisis plan should explicitly include attention to the needs of staff. Policies and procedures should address staff support issues proactively, such as by establishing an employee assistance program.

- Preparing the school to respond effectively to a crisis situation should be seen as just one component of the school's response to a range of mental health and social development efforts. Efforts in school crisis planning should be part of an integrated system that includes prevention and mitigation, intervention, and recovery. Helping children and staff cope with crisis situations not only helps them return more fully to educational tasks, but also helps them later in life to deal with other challenges they may face. This may be one of the most important skills they will learn in school.

THE ROLES AND RESPONSIBILITIES OF CRISIS TEAM MEMBERS

The handbook *How to Prepare for and Respond to a Crisis* (Schonfeld et al., 2002) provides an overview of roles and responsibilities of crisis team members, protocols to follow in crisis situations, and support documents (e.g., draft notification letters, vignettes for tabletop drills). The model employs a team approach (as opposed to vesting all decision making solely with the principal—often an overwhelming burden in the context of a crisis). The following is a list of the major roles, further details of which can be found in the handbook:

- *Crisis team chair*, who is often a school administrator, chairs the scheduled and emergency meetings of the team, oversees the activities of the team members, and serves as the primary liaison with the district-level team.
- *Crisis team assistant chair* (or cochair) assists the chair and substitutes for the chair as needed.
- *Coordinator of counseling services* is a team member with appropriate counseling training and expertise. This individual will help determine the extent and nature of counseling services that may be required during a crisis event and mobilizes counseling resources from both within and outside the school as needed. This individual is also responsible for supervising mental health training and establishing and maintaining liaisons with community mental health providers.
- *The media coordinator* serves as the contact person for the media and prepares, along with other members of

the team, statements for notification of students, staff, and parents, as well as any press releases.

- *The staff notification coordinator* establishes, maintains, and initiates communication systems for notifying crisis team members and other school staff outside of school hours, such as through a telephone tree that is updated on an ongoing basis.
- *The communications coordinator* oversees and conducts in-house communication, such as notification of the entire team of an event during school hours. This individual, who is often the school secretary or other office staff member, screens incoming calls, reads a prepared statement with basic information for relevant callers, and maintains a call log.
- *The crowd management coordinator* develops plans for safe and effective crowd management in the event of a crisis and directly supervises the movement of students and staff if such plans are initiated. This individual will work closely with first responders (e.g., police and fire departments) in the development of these plans and should have a working knowledge of the physical plant.

CONDUCTING A TEAM PLANNING MEETING

There are many ways to conduct a crisis preparedness team planning meeting. One way to begin these meetings is to create a Hierarchy of Safety pyramid that has three levels: the bottom level is labeled Physical Safety; the middle level is Social Safety; and the top layer is Emotional Safety. Such a device is an excellent planning tool in that it helps participants visualize the issues in distinct categories. Participants can use this chart to clarify dangers and plans as well as to visually summarize what the team is already doing on one or more levels, along with what the team needs to plan for and develop.

Normally, when one thinks of a school crisis, one has in mind a wide range of categories: the death of a student and subsequent bereavement; an environmental disaster; firearm incidents in the school. More recently, one thinks of terrorism, an armed intruder, or biological warfare. Participants are encouraged to volunteer their own conceptualizations of what would constitute a crisis— large or small—within the context of their own school setting. The common denominator for responding to all types of crises is the need for an effective leader in the person of the principal, excellent communication skills among the staff, and delegation of responsibilities.

The planning process outlined here is designed to be tailor-made for each school, given its own idiosyncrasies, structure, and culture. Especially in matters pertaining to safety and security, each discipline (teachers, counselors, nurses, custodians, and security staff) and even each individual will have different perspectives and opinions. Differences of opinion are inevitable and are to be expected, especially in times of crisis. Part of the role of the crisis team chair is to moderate these differing opinions and to arrive at some consensus. It is far better that these conflicts emerge during the planning process than during an actual crisis when students are looking to school staff for coherent leadership.

SUMMARY

Making schools safe necessarily includes crisis preparedness planning. Such planning and related prevention efforts that address school safety and security reduce the likelihood that a crisis will occur. Yet crises can and will occur in schools. If a school has developed a thoughtful and sustained crisis preparedness plan, it will dramatically reduce the negative impact of actual crises.

Crisis preparedness planning needs to address physical dangers but also the social emotional needs of students and school personnel. There is a series of procedures, roles, and responsibilities that define effective crisis preparedness planning.

REFLECTING ON YOUR CURRENT PRACTICE

- What does it mean to you to be safe at school?
- How do you define safety within the confines of your own school?
- Feeling safe and being safe are not identical concepts. Are there physical barriers (such as locked doors or gates at the gym) to safety in your school? How could these be eliminated?
- How have terrorist alerts, anxieties provoked by war, or shooting incidents in schools affected your students and staff?
- What are you already doing to make your school safe (1) physically, (2) socially, and (3) emotionally?
- Do you have a team approach to safety and an ongoing process for crisis preparedness?
- What does your school crisis plan delineate? What are the most important details?
- How many people in your school know about the existence of the plan?
- How many people really know what to do?

CHAPTER THREE

Creating a Climate for Social and Emotional Safety

"I have a tummy ache, Mom. I don't want to go to school to-day." As Jack and his mother walked to school, he began to tell her about how some of the older boys were teasing him and his friends. "Mom, Mrs. Smith saw them doing it yesterday, and she did nothing!" Jack tells his mother that Mrs. Smith, a teacher's aide, has told him to "just ignore them." Jack begins to cry. "I can't ignore them. I keep thinking about when they are going to do this again. Mom, I just want to go home."

Feeling safe socially, emotionally, and physically provides the optimal foundation for learning and healthy development. Whether we feel safe or not influences our emotional experiences which in turn influence our social experiences. Because Jack, in the above vignette, was teased yesterday, he will naturally tend to anxiously expect to be teased again today. Or a child who feels emotionally wounded—for example, as the result of a trauma—may act in a victimized manner, which increases the chances of being bullied. There are two core dimensions that enhance the likelihood that children and adults will feel safe in school: (1) creating a caring, participatory, and responsive school climate that values and fosters safety; and (2) actively teaching and promoting students' social emotional competencies and ethical dispositions. In this chapter, the focus is on a series of steps that adults and students alike can take to create a climate of learning and safety, which serves as a primary violence prevention measure and promotes healthy youth development.

A complex set of interactive factors colors how safe we feel and are in school. There are societal factors—for example, the school's reputation and media reports that communities are safe or unsafe. There are community factors—neighborhood exposure to violence, the presence of drugs and alcohol, the sense of belonging to a community. There are family factors—the quality of parent-child relationships. There are school climate factors—the explicit rules and the hidden rules, the relationships between adults and youth. And very important, and perhaps the chief factor: how connected the student feels to at least one adult in the school building (Blum, McNeely, & Rinehart, 2002; Catalano, Haggerty, Oesterie, Fleming, & Hawkins, 2004; Karcher, 2002a, 2002b; Kirby, 2001; Whitlock, 2006).

There is a hierarchy of safety needs. Physical safety is foundational. If we feel unsafe physically, it is more difficult and often simply irrelevant to consider social and emotional dimensions. To the extent that we do feel safe physically, it is important for school personnel to consider how we can promote students'—and adults'—sense of social and emotional safety. Promoting students' experience of feeling safe socially and emotionally enhances their ability to learn, to establish friendships, and to develop in healthy ways (Cohen, 2001).

Clearly, in the opening vignette, Mrs. Smith's advice to just ignore the bullies is not very helpful. In this chapter, we focus on three overlapping interventions that can enable educators to create safer and more caring, participatory, and responsive classrooms and schools:

1. Developing a comprehensive school safety plan that is based on collaborative dialogue among educators, parents, and students about what kind of school they want, with a resulting set of short-term and longer-term goals.
2. Coordinating existing health promotion, risk prevention, and SEL/CE efforts.
3. Working to create smaller learning communities.

DEVELOPING A COMPREHENSIVE SCHOOL SAFETY PLAN

Virtually all schools have a comprehensive school safety plan. However, these plans often focus on physical safety planning alone. Creating a truly effective and comprehensive school plan necessarily rests on a collaborative, schoolwide process of school personnel, parents, and students working and learning together to understand how safe they feel already, the efficacy of current efforts, and a collaboratively developed vision of what they want the school to be.

There is a series of steps that schools in conjunction with parent associations (and optimally, key stakeholders in the community) need to take together to develop a shared vision and a related shared vocabulary. This collaborative planning creates the foundation for reflection, implementation, and the ongoing process of evaluation and related readjustment of implementation efforts. Two specific dimensions are particularly important in the development of a socially and emotionally informed comprehensive school safety plan: developing and implementing a positive behavioral support system and developing 1-year or 2-year themes that shape ongoing vocabulary and reflection.

Implementing Positive Behavioral Support Systems

To a greater or lesser extent, all schools utilize a problem-solving model to identify problems and positive goals and develop related plans. These efforts vary in a number of ways. Are they coordinated? To what extent have key stakeholders had an opportunity to contribute to these plans? Are they evidence based? Are they effective? It is important to develop evidence-based systems to identify students who are out of control as well as at risk and an ongoing method of evaluating to what extent the school is successfully addressing these students' needs. This process represents an essential component of a comprehensive school safety plan. This schoolwide dimension overlaps with the model and process that we detail in Chapter 8. Too often, schools focus only on problems and do not also develop positive or prosocial goals. Whether it is 5% or 20% of the student body that is out of control, reacting to these crises too often becomes the ongoing job for educational administrators, counselors, and teachers. *Zero tolerance* is the phrase that has described America's response to student misbehavior. Zero tolerance means that a school will automatically and severely punish a student for any number of safety-related infractions (ERIC, 2001). Zero tolerance also reducess the authority of the principal, whose hands are tied by mandated policies. He or she is often unable to exercise discretion in highly complex cases or to deal with incidents in a prudent way. An American Psychological Association task force reviewed 10 years of research on the effects of zero tolerance policies and concluded that these programs not only fail to make schools safer but can increase the incidence of problem behaviors and dropout rates (Farberman, 2006; see also Black, 2004).

In recent years, more attention has been paid to how we can set up evidence-based systems that allow participants—from the individual to the school to the community—to identify areas of concern or need, determine existing resources and skills, identify possible inhibitors and enablers to system change, institute plans for positive change, and evaluate ongoing change efforts (Nakasato, 2000; Sprague & Walker, 2000). A technical assistance center on positive behavioral interventions and support has been established by the Office of Special Education Programs, U.S. Department of Education, to give schools capacity-building information and assistance for identifying, adapting, and sustaining effective schoolwide disciplinary practices (see www.pbis.org/).

Developing Themes That Shape Vocabulary and Ongoing Reflection

When school personnel and parents reflect upon and review past safety efforts and begin to develop a shared vision about next steps, an important and linked goal is the development of a shared vocabulary. How are we going to talk about our goals? The language we use shapes how we think. And how we think shapes behavior. For example, when many people in the school begin to use similar language (e.g., about the importance of tolerance or actively standing up to bully-victim behavior or being a passive bystander), these ideas become part of how we think. Let's think for a moment about Jack in the vignette at the beginning of the chapter. If the teachers, parents, and students in his school had decided to focus on the bully-victim-bystander cycle, Jack and his mother would have wondered why the teachers' aide did not stand up and say, "I am uncomfortable with this bullying behavior" or "That bullying is not acceptable."

When we have a shared vision and a shared vocabulary, it creates a platform for ongoing reflection and learning. For example, if an important goal is to support all members of the school community to actively stand up when they see bully-victim behavior and develop a series of scripts that children and adults can use, it becomes very easy to spend 5 minutes at the end of each day in class reflecting on bully-victim-bystander behavior. A typical script might begin, "Let's talk for a few minutes about today's incident. Whether or not we recognized bully-victim behavior when it was happening, whether or not we were able to actively stand up to bully-victim behavior, let's learn from whatever happened." This kind of ongoing reflective learning may be one of the single most powerful ways that we can promote social emotional learning and effect behavioral change.

COORDINATING EXISTING EFFORTS

One important systemic intervention that fosters socially and emotionally as well as physically safe schools is to coordinate existing risk prevention, health promotion, and SEL/CE efforts. Research has affirmed that the essential foundation for efforts in all of these areas is (1) systemic interventions that create a safer, more caring, participatory, and responsive school and community; and

(2) promoting students' social and emotional competencies in an ongoing, collaborative manner.

Virtually all schools have any number of programmatic efforts designed to foster a sense of safety and connectedness. For example, all schools have health education classes, violence prevention, and safe and drug-free efforts, and most include cooperative learning and conflict resolution efforts. However, these efforts are typically fragmented and uncoordinated. The educators involved with these overlapping efforts often do not talk together about the following questions:

- What are our goals for a given semester or year?
- What are the specific skills, knowledge, and beliefs that we are seeking to promote now?
- What vocabulary will we emphasize? How might we develop a shared vocabulary?
- How we can mutually reinforce overlapping efforts in these areas?
- How can we evaluate our efforts in ways that will both further our own adult understanding of what is working and show students how we all need to be ongoing, reflective learners?

This process is not complicated or expensive. It does mean that the coordinators of health promotion, risk prevention, and SEL/CE efforts need to meet periodically and address the questions noted above.

WORKING TO CREATE SMALLER LEARNING COMMUNITIES

A growing body of research underscores the intuitively common-sense notion that smaller schools provide a more stable environment for students as they move through the school years as well as for students who need a more individualized approach. The Web site located at http://www.whatkidscando.org/ presents students' own perspectives on the most desirable or practical ways to redesign high schools. This is primary school violence prevention at its best.

Large schools and districts face enormous pressures—the need to accommodate growing numbers of recent immigrants, the need to continue to utilize outmoded buildings, and, almost everywhere, the need to get along with smaller budgets. But more and more groups of teachers and administrators are no longer willing to live with these bigger schools with populations of 3,000 to 5,000 students and their antiquated governance structures which do not facilitate academic learning or provide the stable milieu and individualized attention that students need to cope with the postmodern culture that surrounds them. It is much more likely that children like Jack will feel alone and isolated in large schools. Research shows that when schools are smaller, it is more likely that students will feel connected to at least one adult in the building. So Jack could have talked to an adult about being bullied. All of the indicators point to the need to construct smaller learning communities as the ideal way to foster social and emotional growth, academic achievement, and a real sense of school security.

Small schools are not a cure-all for all the ills of the education system, but when they are operating at their best they offer students one-on-one attention and create situations in which students can feel that it is safe to ask questions and demonstrate their interest in academic subjects. When students feel that they are well known and appreciated socially, emotionally, and academically, they feel safer and more confident, and are more inclined to perform altruistic acts.

The nationwide movement is now experimenting with multiple ways of constructing smaller learning communities:

- Downsizing huge schools of 3,000 students into ten smaller schools of 300
- Creating a new school at the sixth grade level and adding one grade a year
- Designing smaller, autonomous "schools within schools" in the same building

- Attaching schools to museums, hospitals, even zoos
- Partnering high schools with universities and offering college credits

The common goal of all these approaches is to enable students to spend their school days in an open, stress-free environment. Clearly, not every school will be able to create such an ambiance for its students and its staff, certainly not overnight. Our point in highlighting the small-schools approach here is that it represents one very important example of primary prevention of school violence. Structural violence—or symbolic violence, as it is sometimes called—is the violence that inheres in institutions even when real physical or emotional violence is not present. Allowing our minority populations to persist decade after decade in poverty is one example of structural violence. Allowing the overcrowded large high schools, which are relics of an earlier industrial age, to continue to exist is another example of structural violence. These are literally time bombs waiting to explode in violence. Students feel alienated and anxious as they walk the poorly supervised corridors.

SUMMARY

Promoting students' experience of feeling socially and emotionally safe enhances learning and healthy development. There is a series of specific steps that school leaders can take to actualize this goal. At the level of individual students, we need to develop systems to recognize and address the needs of troubled youths. Students in dire need will signal, directly or indirectly, that they are in trouble until someone engages them. Two common ways that these students signal their need for help is to act out and hurt others or to "act in" and become self-destructive. School leaders need to consider to what extent they are teaching students specific social and emotional skills that promote reflective, empathic, problem solving, communication, and collaborative capacities. These are the underlying skills that support students talking about and meeting healthy needs as well as recognizing other students who may be signaling that they are in trouble. These skills provide an essential foundation for sustained and effective violence prevention work in schools. Finally, school leaders need to think systemically about how to make the school community a safe place where people can tell the truth and learn to be "upstanders" (see Chapter 6 for details). These systemic interventions and processes create the foundation for effective violence prevention efforts.

Typically, the social and emotional dimensions of feeling safe influence one another interactively. Social experience (e.g., being teased) affects internal emotional experience (e.g., "I am worried I will be teased again"). Positive social experiences (e.g., "People stand up for me when I am being teased") affect emotional experience (e.g., "I feel people care about me") as well as ensuing social behavior (e.g., "People have stood up for me and now I will want to stand up for others"). And our emotional experiences (e.g., "I feel strong and have a good group of friends") shape our social behavior (e.g., "I will stand up and tell that bully to stop being mean").

Children do not feel safe when they see violence on a regular basis, either in their neighborhoods or at school. Feeling safe is clearly related to the effectiveness of public safety (the police) in keeping overt violence in a community at a low level. Even in middle-class neighborhoods, young people are exposed to a culture of violence through the media, the entertainment industry, and the casual acceptance of violence—what is known as the normalization of violence. Many seemingly ordinary features of our culture contribute to this desensitization. For example, school metal detectors, although they may be necessary for a number of reasons, also convey the message that violence is normal and is to be expected.

Many school attendance problems and truancy problems have their basis in students' desire to avoid hostile conflicts. One key factor in making a student feel safe consists simply of having a safe place (an office, an activity room, a safe after-school program) to go to both during and after school. Feeling safe is also related to the social climate in a school: When students are encouraged to engage in altruistic behaviors (helping other students, counseling), academic performance improves and students feel safer. The presence of a meaningful relationship with a single adult is one of the key factors in feeling safe. One of the most powerful forces in schools is the presence of mentors.

Many kids feel that they are academic failures and do not believe that it is emotionally safe to keep on trying. Some students—both boys and girls—will tease a student who is trying to cooperate with the teacher, volunteering information, or raising questions. Schools need to have a clear policy that they will not tolerate teasing or putdowns.

The following approaches represent research-based systemic interventions that tend to foster a safer, more caring, participatory, and responsive school climate:

- Fostering teacher-parent-student discussions and related action planning about what kind of school they want. This dialogue can create a schoolwide ethos that fosters positive discipline, academic success, and social and emotional wellness.
- Assessing what is being done that is effective and ascertaining that efforts are not being duplicated.
- Explicitly stating that the school community values and is committed to fostering a sense of social, emotional, and physical safety.
- Parents, teachers, and optimally students deciding on year-long themes (e.g., the bully-victim-bystander cycle) that provide ongoing opportunities to reflect and learn about what promotes or inhibits safety and learning.
- Working to create smaller learning communities.
- Working to ensure that every student feels connected to at least one adult in the school building.
- Coordinating existing risk prevention and health promotion efforts.

- Identifying at-risk students from the pre-K level on and intervene with the 10–15% of students who are at risk for severe academic or behavioral problems through an identification process developed by the building-level student support team.
- Eliminating bullying by actively addressing bullying, victim, and bystander behaviors and teaching students to recognize such behavior.
- Promoting tolerance by teaching students to understand issues of diversity.
- Being positive role models for students; solving problems with colleagues nonviolently and respectfully.

REFLECTING ON YOUR CURRENT PRACTICE

- Do students tell adults when they feel unsafe in school?
- Are rules for student behavior clearly communicated?
- Are rules for student behavior consistently and fairly administered?
- Is there a shared sense of responsibility among adults for student discipline?
- To what extent do students have a shared sense of responsibility for student discipline?
- Do teachers have input regarding the school discipline policy?
- Do students have input regarding the school discipline policy?
- To what extent do teachers address problems with student behavior in a positive, proactive manner? To what extent has professional development fostered this?
- To what extent are rules and regulations reasonable?
- To what extent do students feel socially and emotionally comfortable in school?
- Are teachers and staff trained to recognize student at-risk behaviors?

- Are children who demonstrate at-risk behaviors identified and assisted in the area of effective problem solving?
- Are students with emotional problems referred to and followed up by mental health personnel?
- Is there ongoing professional development for teachers on topics related to effective discipline, bullying, and school climate?
- To what extent is the school working to create smaller learning communities?
- Do you agree that smaller is better? What are the implications of this adage in your own academic setting?
- Many student disruption and suspension issues could be better addressed if schools could provide one-on-one or small-group learning settings for students. How can individualized or small-group interactions be better promoted within your school?
- To what extent do the adults in the school building work to be active and positive social emotional learning role models?
- To what extent is there an ongoing reflective discussion in the school about diversity, in-group and out-group behavior, and the importance of being tolerant?
- To what extent are the adults committed to ongoing assessment so that they can learn about what is and is not working in these areas? How is this being done?

CHAPTER FOUR

Promoting Social Emotional Competencies and Healthy Relationships

> Johnny and Robby's Spanish teacher threw them out of class because while Robby was reading a passage out loud from the text, he came upon a suggestive word and he and Johnny started laughing uncontrollably. The teacher yelled at them and they stopped, but she was so irritated that she called the security guard and had them removed. "For no reason, for no reason," Johnny and Robby insisted when they were being led down the corridor by the security guard. The guard took the pair down to the conflict resolution class, where the teacher said, "OK, what happened, guys?" "She's a bitch and I'm gonna hurt her. I'm going to get her after school and slash her. She deserves it," Johnny replied. "Oh, great, Johnny. You're going to let some teacher mess up the rest of your life?" "I don't care. It'll make me feel better."

In this chapter, we focus on the second core dimension of social and emotional safety that enhances the likelihood that children and adults will feel safe in school: direct teaching and learning that enhances social emotional competencies and ethical dispositions. Longitudinal and psychoeducational research has identified a set of core social emotional competencies that can predict children's ability to learn and solve conflicts in nonviolent ways (Cohen, 2001; Fuchs et al., 2002; Weissberg & Greenberg, 1998). In Johnny's case, for example, the adults may begin to relate to him in a one-on-one setting where he will be able to think through and work through his violent fantasies and begin to appreciate how self-destructive they are. These same competencies enhance the likelihood that children will be more inclined to recognize others in distress and to actively take steps to respond to problems rather than being passive bystanders who inadvertently contribute to a climate of fear in the school (Collaborative for Academic, Social and Emotional Learning, 2003; Slaby, Wilson-Brewer, & Dash, 1994; Twemlow, Fonagy, Sacco, Gies, & Hess, 2001). Learning to become more socially and emotionally literate complements and extends the systemic dimension of social emotional safety described in Chapter 3.

Just as educators and parents can intentionally promote children's ability to decode phonemes and then use this information to become lifelong language learners, we can promote children's ability to decode their social selves and their relationships to others (their reflective and empathic abilities), and then learn to use this information to become lifelong social emotional learners.

The degree to which we are able to promote such learning can predict life satisfaction and productivity, whereas grades and SAT scores, by themselves, cannot (Bar-On, 2005; Goleman, 1995; Heath, 1991; Valliant, 1977). In fact, social and emotional competencies are predictive of adolescents and adults' ability to form and maintain healthy relationships, to work effectively (Goleman, 1998), and even to age well (Valliant, 2002). Learning to become more socially and emotionally literate complements and extends the systemic dimension of social emotional safety described in Chapter 3.

In this chapter, we detail these core social and emotional competencies: reflective, empathic, problem-solving, and decision-making skills as well as cooperative, communicative, self-motivational, friendship-related and altruistic skills, knowledge, and beliefs. We also detail the range of ways that school personnel can promote these essential life skills. When we promote students' social and emotional competencies, we are enhancing healthy development as well as taking meaningful steps to prevent risky behavior. For example, Johnny's inability to recognize his frustration could inadvertently result in his getting into even more serious trouble. Clearly, Johnny had not had a chance to learn and practice paying attention to his underlying emotions (e.g., frustration) and needs (e.g., that the teacher recognize that he was not trying to disrupt the class). We now turn to these core social and emotional competencies and the range of ways that we can integrate social emotional education into school life.

CORE SOCIAL AND EMOTIONAL COMPETENCIES

In this section, we focus on the core social and emotional competencies that parents and educators can promote in the classrooms and hallways of schools as well as in homes. Although different longitudinal researchers have used somewhat different terms, our listing of competencies represents an organization of social emotional skills that leading psychosocial researchers and practitioners have endorsed (Fuchs-Nadeau et al., 2002). (Note that these competencies were the foundation for New York State's interpersonal violence prevention guidelines.) For each competency, we begin with a brief definition and overview; offer guidelines that help children to learn these sets of skills, knowledge, and beliefs; and conclude with a series of examples and tips about teaching and learning.

Reflective and Empathic Abilities: Connecting With Ourselves and Others

Definition and overview. Learning to connect or listen to ourselves (reflective capacities) and others (empathic capacities) is the foundation for social emotional competency (Cohen, 2001). This capacity involves learning to listen actively to verbal and nonverbal messages and to think about what they mean. It also means recognizing when we do not understand what another person is saying or what we ourselves are saying or feeling, thereby honoring (rather than masking) our confusion. Listening to others and ourselves provides the social emotional information we need to make decisions, solve conflicts nonviolently, cooperate, communicate, and form friendships.

Feeling connected to ourselves and others and experiencing self-awareness is an essential facet of creating safe schools for several reasons:

- People who are violent—be it physically, socially, or emotionally—are typically disconnected from themselves. Anger and rage typically grow out of frustration and loss. When children as well as adults are disconnected due to feelings of frustration and loss, they are more likely to act in violent ways.
- When a student is feeling aggressive and vulnerable to acting violently, sensing that others are listening and wanting to understand how he or she is feeling, in supportive ways, reduces the likelihood that he or she will act violently.
- Students who feel connected to other students are more likely to express support and caring. This is the kind of social environment that promotes safety and discourages violence as a solution to problems. It is also the type of social environment that allows and encourages students to confide in adults regarding a fellow student they may be concerned about.

Guidelines.   There are a number of organizing guidelines that can enhance educators' and parents' ability to connect with children.

- Be curious about children's experiences.
- Ask questions to learn more about children's experiences.
- Listen, listen, and listen.
- Recognize and honor children's experiences. We do not need to always agree with or be pleased with what children say, but it is useful to recognize and honor their experiences.
- Do not tell children that they should not feel a certain way when they are beginning to express feelings—be

it verbally, artistically, or otherwise. On the other hand, there are many other moments when it is essential that we let children know what they should and should not do.

- Display an appreciative attitude. With few exceptions, children do the best they can. Even when a child misbehaves, this typically occurs because the child does not think he or she has any other options. An appreciative attitude can powerfully foster our ability to connect with others. Recognizing that children try to do their best enhances their ability to be open to adults' suggestions and comments.

- Accept confusion and not knowing. Children have a common belief that it is unacceptable to be confused or not know the answer. Although this misunderstanding tends to become more prevalent as children move into middle and high school, it often begins in the first years of school life. As we detail in Chapter 5, parents and educators have a series of ongoing opportunities to let children know it is normal to be confused and not know the answers. In fact, these are wonderful opportunities to learn something new if we allow ourselves to ask for help.

- Pay attention to feeling unable to connect. When we have difficulty connecting with a child, it may be an important signal that something is amiss. If you are concerned about not being able to connect with a child, confer with your school administrator, school counselor, or other community members who have expertise in these areas.

- Allow children to express even their most angry feelings or most destructive fantasies. Help them think about these images and ideas by projecting the possible future negative consequences for these actions.

Examples and tips. What follows is a series of examples and tips that can support our capacity to connect with children and foster social emotional learning to prevent youth violence:

- Ask questions. "How would you feel if you were in that person's shoes? How are you feeling right now?"
- Acknowledge. "We have a problem. What do you think our goal should be? What are the range of ways we can solve this problem?"
- Learn and listen. "What matters to you? How can we learn more about that?"
- Tell stories about how you learned these skills, understandings, and beliefs. It is very important to include stories about moments when we had trouble learning one or more of these capacities. This gives children permission to talk about what is difficult or confusing. As adults, we often shield our children from difficult social emotional moments in our lives. We do not want to burden our children. Yet this can sometimes inadvertently contribute to children thinking that life is easy for us and that we never have problems.
- Make social emotional learning a part of what you do at home and in the classroom. In the classroom, at the dinner table, or in the car, there are many moments when we can think about how we are feeling and how the other person is feeling; what the problem is and what our goal is in facing a given decision or problem; what our options are and what would be the best ways to tackle a situation; what we really want to say to a person; how we might cooperate with others; how we might reach out to that person whom we would like to get to know more.
- Pay attention to the match between the child and the environment (home or classroom). We all come into the world with a "biological package" or temperament. Shyness, activity levels, and soothability are just a few of the many temperamental dimensions that researchers have learned about in recent years. One of the important factors that can inadvertently complicate a child's level of connectedness is a poor match between the environment (home or classroom) and the child's disposition. For example, some teachers insist that young children learn to sit still in their classrooms be-

fore they are ready. A poor match often contributes to children pulling back and disconnecting.

- Recognize changes. As our children grow physically, socially, and emotionally, it is important to recognize and explicitly acknowledge these changes. Recognizing and validating these changes provides a foundation for connectedness. A wonderful way to talk about these kinds of changes is to tell children stories about ourselves when we were children. Sometimes telling stories about our own changes without explicitly asking or suggesting that they should talk about their own changes allows them to be more comfortable and open up. For example, the passage into adolescence, which often begins well before the ninth grade, involves a series of extraordinary physical, mental, social, and emotional changes. In conjunction with the very visible physical changes that accompany puberty and the new mental capacities that many adolescents show, we often see children becoming more independent and moving away from parents and teachers. However, the need to be connected to others and ourselves is as important as ever.

Problem-Solving and Decision-Making Abilities

Definition and overview. Life involves a series of decisions and problems. How we solve problems and make choices shapes our lives and our ability to handle conflicts in nonviolent ways. Flexible and healthy decision making and problem solving involves engaging in a process of weighing options and consequences and coming to a conclusion that will result in positive and productive behavior. This competency includes the ability to develop and implement a plan, evaluate successes and barriers, and revise the plan to accomplish the objectives effectively.

Guidelines. There are helpful and unhelpful ways to solve problems and make decisions. It is useful to teach children the steps that characterize flexible and creative problem solving and decision making.

A primary approach in learning to solve problems and to enhance decision-making abilities in children is to use a specific model. It is important to remember that for children to use this model, adults should be modeling this behavior and technique in their everyday life. Here is one example of an effective tool for problem solving and decision making and planning:

1. Make a clear statement of what the problem is. Define the problem.
2. Consider possible solutions to the problem. What can we do to fix it?
3. Test and evaluate these conclusions and arrive at a solution.
4. Take action and implement the best solution.
5. Evaluate the results of the action. Did the plan work?

Examples and tips. Here are some examples and tips that may support your teaching children these essential violence prevention skills, understandings, and beliefs:

- Talk about "good" and "not-so-good" problems: Normalize the notion that life is a series of problems and decisions and that the key issue is how we can become flexible and creative problem solvers.
- Talk about times when we did not solve problems so well. This can allow children to reflectively consider their own helpful and not-so-helpful problem-solving strategies.
- Underscore the importance of learning to recognize our emotional state and to keep calm. This is one of the foundations for helpful problem-solving abilities.
- Be a learner with children. Whatever happens when they (or we) are faced with a problem or decision can become a teachable moment, an opportunity to reflect and think about how we might have managed this if we could do it over again.

- Appreciate and practice goal-setting, the first critical stage in the problem-solving process. How we set goals (automatically or thoughtfully) is important. Goals drive behavior.

One of the very important decisions that children make pertains to acceptable and unacceptable ways to settle conflicts and disputes. Researchers have found that it is especially important to help middle school children (ages 6 to 11) learn about this skill (Huesmann, Guerra, Miller, & Zelli, 1992; Selman, Beardslee, Schultz, Krupa, & Podoresky, 1986). Helping children understand that it is not necessary to use physical force to settle disputes and to develop related skills and knowledge about how to manage interpersonal disputes is an important step in the creation of socially and emotionally as well as physically safe schools.

Communicative Capacities

Definition and overview. Communicative capacities refer to our ability to express ourselves and be clearly understood and our ability to understand what is being verbally and nonverbally transmitted back. Research has shown that fostering clear communication between children and adults is an important component of interpersonal violence prevention and the creation of safe schools (Pianta, 1999). It contributes to children feeling more connected and less isolated from others. How we communicate parents or educators becomes the model for how children communicate. Learning to put our feelings into words reduces the likelihood that we will feel frustrated and act aggressively or violently. Learning to communicate clearly and directly includes the ability to use refusal skills, assertiveness, and verbal as well as nonverbal methods to engage in positive behavior. Helping children to acquire observational, listening, and other communication skills reduces conflict and helps children handle problems more easily. If adults use inappropriate expressions and verbal put-downs, children will see these as acceptable forms of communication.

Guidelines. Communicating clearly and directly is hard work, and it is an ongoing process. Pay attention to how your children communicate and recognize their efforts. Think about what kind of communicator you are: Our actions become a model for our children.

Examples and tips. What follows is a number of examples and tips that can aid our efforts to foster this fundamentally important skill and understanding:

- Learn to listen. Pay attention to what the child is saying; find time to be alone with the child; do not interrupt; do not prepare your response while your child is speaking; reserve making judgments or decisions or arriving at conclusions and solutions until the child has finished speaking.
- Look at and observe the child. Be aware of the child's facial expressions and body language. Is the child nervous and uncomfortable, or relaxed and happy? Reading these signs will help adults know how the child is feeling and respond more appropriately. During the conversation, acknowledge what the child is saying and move close to the child, make eye contact, and nod.
- Encourage respect for individual differences. If you are tolerant of people who are different from you, then the child will be more likely to model your behavior.
- Teach children, beginning at an early age, the importance of learning to say no or take a time-out when they feel uncomfortable.
- Respond and recognize. Use "I-statements" to let the child know how you feel about what he or she is saying. Speak for yourself and do not try to put words into the child's mouth. Identify when it is important for you to tell the child what you believe about a topic or issue and when it would be better for the child to figure out what he or she believes without your opinion. I-messages are simple, powerful ways to communicate our wants, needs, and feelings. By teaching chil-

dren to use these messages, you are giving them tools to help them in situations where they need to feel empowered and listened to.

Impulse Control and Anger Management (Self-Management, Stress Management, and Self-Regulation)

Definition and overview. Impulse control and anger management refer to our ability to recognize when we are feeling impulsive or angry and manage these urges in appropriate, nonviolent ways. Research has shown that learning how to control one's impulses will reduce violent behavior (Guerra, 2003). Anger is one of the most difficult emotions for children to manage. When children are angry, it is difficult for them to think clearly and make appropriate choices. In the vignette at the beginning of the chapter, Johnny was certainly not thinking clearly when he fantasized knifing the teacher who disciplined him. This is why it is an important violence prevention strategy for children—beginning in the prekindergarten years—to learn about and practice impulse control and anger management. Research has shown that learning to control impulses at an early age reduces the likelihood of aggressive and violent behavior in adolescence (Zigler, Styfco, & Gilman, 1993).

Guidelines. Learning to control our impulses rests on our ability to recognize our emotional state, contain these impulses, and find safe and appropriate ways to express them. It is important for children to understand that it is okay to feel angry or impulsive. However, children need to learn that there are acceptable and unacceptable ways to express these impulses. It is also useful for children to gradually learn that anger typically stems from frustration or loss.

Examples and tips. What follows is a series of ideas, examples, and tips that can further your ability to help children learn to recognize and manage their impulses:

- Label emotions, your own and others. This helps children to develop a vocabulary of feelings. If we can talk about our feelings, it is easier to recognize and manage them.
- Practice recognizing the physical signs or cues that accompany anger and other strong feelings. For example, the following questions can spur important discussion and discovery about this: How does your body feel when you are angry? What do your hands do? What does your face do? How does your voice sound? Do you walk, sit, or stand differently?
- Talk about "okay" and "not so okay" ways to express strong impulses.
- Help children understand that anger typically grows out of frustration or hurt.
- In class and at home, engage in conversations about what children should do when they are feeling angry or hurt.
- Talk about the various ways that we manage feeling frustrated and hurt, both helpful and unhelpful.
- Acknowledge a child's feelings. For example, say, "I can see you are angry." "It looks like you are pretty mad about . . . " This is important because many children calm down quickly when they realize someone recognizes how they are feeling.
- To help children understand what triggers anger, you can ask them to make statements like, "I get angry when . . . "
- Teach children how to keep calm. Generate a list of ways that a child can stay calm. Refer to the list when the child gets angry.

Cooperative Capacities

Definition and overview. *Cooperating* refers to our capacity to work together in pairs and groups. Being able to listen, take turns, and develop collaborative goals and strategies to accomplish these goals is an essential set of skills and knowledge that provides the foundation for this ability. Research has shown that cooperation is a core competency that allows us to develop healthy friendships and positive relationships throughout life (Johnson & Johnson, 1989).

When children cooperate, they learn to appreciate the strengths and differences of each classmate or family member. They also learn to wait and take turns. This creates an atmosphere of acceptance, tolerance, and respect. When children play and work together, the environment is less competitive because the goal of cooperation is success of the group or family rather than the individual.

Organizing guidelines. Being able to cooperate is pleasurable and meaningful. It is also hard work. The capacity to cooperate rests on a number of social and emotional skills and understandings that include active listening; impulse control and the ability to take turns; identifying and setting goals; appreciating what others are thinking and doing; contributing new ideas; being able to ask for help, accept help, and help others; taking responsibility for one's actions; and working toward a shared goal.

Examples and tips. What follows is a series of examples and tips that can further our ability to teach and learn about this core competency:

- When we have a cooperative opportunity, acknowledge it. Be explicit about cooperation as an important and sometimes difficult process.
- Encourage children to ask for help when they are having a problem in an interaction. Asking for help is not an admission of failure, but it identifies that there is a problem that needs to be solved.
- Ask questions. What is the problem? What have you tried to do to solve the problem already? How do you want me to help?
- Encourage children to look at a situation as a problem to be solved rather than as a question of who is to

blame. If the child sees that you do not put value on blame, then it will not be an issue in the future.

- Suggest possible solutions when a child is stuck, and try to give the child choices so that he or she feels empowered.
- After a cooperative exercise or experience, talk about what it was like. What was easy? What was difficult? How can we learn from it?

Ability to Form Friendships

Definition and overview. The ability to form friendships rests on many other social and emotional competencies: being able to listen to ourselves and the other person; being able to control our impulses; and being able to communicate and cooperate. Research has shown that forming friendships is essential for children's healthy development and happiness (Parker, Rubin, Price, & De-Rosier, 1995; Selman, 2003). Friendships provide a needed sense of belonging for children and adults alike. Friends offer security and support and are important in times of difficulty. Without friends, individuals can develop negative, antisocial behaviors. Researchers have reaffirmed the importance of a stable peer group in early adolescence (ages 12 to 14; Allen, Weissberg, & Hawkins, 1989), and to what extent this group is primarily prosocial or antisocial affects the probability of aggressive and violent behavior. Positive, supportive friendships permit children to deal effectively with risky and negative life situations.

A key factor in helping children build friendships is understanding why one child likes or dislikes interacting and playing with another child. What do the children like to do together? Who is the leader, and who is the follower? Do they prefer one-on-one interactions or enjoy group play more often?

Guidelines. Learning to be a friend is one of the most important capacities we can develop. We need to help children value good friendships and develop the skills and understandings that provide the platform for healthy, supportive, and caring relation-ships. Being a friend is fun; however, as children move into the elementary school years, being a friend also takes time and energy.

Examples and tips. What follows is a series of examples and tips that can further parents' ability to teach and learn about this core competency:

- Learn who a child's friends are.
- Get to know the parents or caregivers of the children.
- Talk about the importance of friendship and the plea-sure of getting to know all different kinds of people in the world.
- Provide the child with an opportunity to get to know his or her friend in the child's home.
- Help the child assess the negative and positive quali-ties of his or her friendships.
- Encourage open communication about friendships.
- Encourage the child to be an individual and not to try to be like his or her friends.
- Help the child to learn to say no in a friendship while still maintaining the friendship.
- Help the child to learn when the friendship is un-healthy and harmful to his or her self-esteem.

Ability to Recognize and Appreciate Diversity and Differences

Definition and overview. Younger children are trying to build an understanding of the world around them. Their interest in ex-ploring who they are makes them aware of the differences and similarities in others around them. They may notice gender, age, color, or physical differences in people.

Children are often victimized by peers because of their sexual orientation or their confusion about their sexual or gender iden-tity. Lesbian, gay, bisexual, and transgendered youth who attend

both public and independent schools are often harassed relent-
lessly and sometimes physically attacked.

By learning to acknowledge differences without bias, children
help create an environment where each child can feel comfortable
about his or her differences and feel safe taking risks or being an
individual in a group. Some skills associated with appreciating
differences are identifying differences and similarities in a nonjudgmental way; using appropriate language to acknowledge or
ask questions about differences; learning to be assertive or to
stand up for themselves or others; building empathy about others'
feelings. Differences can lead to conflict. Children need to learn to
appreciate human differences as enriching rather than threatening. The more children understand about prejudice and discrimi-
nation, the more they will be able to resist prejudice themselves.

Guidelines. Both children and adults make prejudgments
(prejudice) about others. It is useful to recognize how and when
we do this. It is important to learn that if someone is different,
this does not mean that the person is bad. People who are different often evoke anxiety and fear. Teasing and bullying are one
way that some children negatively manage this anxiety and fear.

Examples and tips. Some examples and tips for building these
skills follow:

- Acknowledge differences. The more children hear that
  adults are comfortable with differences and the more
  you discuss this with respect and ease, the more they
  will be able to accept differences.
- Recognize that one common reaction to the other person being different is anxiety.
- Use culturally diverse teaching materials. Post pictures
  around the classroom that depict people from diverse
  backgrounds interacting with each other. It is also helpful to post pictures of people with a variety of body
  types and physical abilities.
- Create diverse groups. Make a conscious effort to put

children from different backgrounds in small groups together. Research has shown that working in small, cooperative groups is an effective way to help young people overcome fears and stereotypes (Johnson & Johnson, 1989).
- Involve families in your curriculum. Celebrate different holidays and traditions in your classroom and have people from each religion or culture explain the holiday or tradition to the class.
- Foster inclusion. Take time to celebrate each child as an important member of the group.

Altruistic Capacities

Definition and overview. Altruistic capacities refers to people's inclination to be concerned about and helpful toward others.

Guidelines. The capacity and inclination to be helpful toward others is one of the organizing processes that fosters safer schools. It is important to remember that empathy can be used in helpful (i.e., altruistic) or unhelpful (i.e., antisocial) ways. For example, when a child empathizes with someone who has inadvertently hurt his or her feelings, it promotes essential social and emotional capacities like maintaining friendships. But when children learn to empathize with the ability to manipulate their peers, this undermines friendships and trust. As is the case with all of the core social emotional competencies described here, the capacity to be altruistic is shaped by a constellation of social emotional skills, knowledge, and values. For example, to be altruistic, children need to be able to actively listen to others, to empathize and reflect, and to be creative social emotional problem solvers. Children need to understand that healthy social relations rest on our helping as well as being helped by others. And the belief or value that helping others is a social responsibility supports the development of this core social emotional competency.

Like all competencies, altruism and the capacity to act in prosocial ways develop over time. Altruistic behaviors have been observed in children as young as 2 years of age. As maturation results in new capacities, children's abilities in these areas blossom. For example, when verbal skills develop in the early elementary school years, children's ability to understand others, to connect, and to help others increases. In early adolescence, the development of greater abstract capacities (which enhances our ability put ourselves in the other person's shoes) dramatically promotes children's ability to empathize with others and thereby be helpful to others.

Examples and tips. The following are examples and tips to aid our efforts to build altruistic capacities in children:

- Be a role model. How do you show that you are helpful to others? Talk about this. There is pleasure in helping others. Let your children or students discover this themselves.
- Provide opportunities for older children to help younger children (e.g., mentoring programs).
- Talk about the pleasures of giving and receiving help. To the extent that there is a balance in our lives, both are important and pleasurable facets of life.
- Discuss world and local events to identify concrete ways for children to express concern and help others.
- Encourage community service and provide opportunities for children to feel and be responsible for others and the environment, such as community trash clean-up, raking leaves for neighbors, and so on. As we detail even more below, service learning or programs that link community service with academic learning provide powerful ways to promote altruistic capacities and social emotional learning.
- When a classmate or friend is absent due to illness, provide help by having a classmate call, take projects to the child, or make a visit, checking first with the child's family.

- Discuss bullying and the importance of children standing together to assist the victim, and to help the bully change behaviors.
- Foster altruistic class projects (e.g., class adopts an orphan in a third world country, raises money for him or her, and corresponds regularly).
- Discuss ways to orient new children and teachers to the school or neighborhood and improve acceptance of diversity and tolerance (i.e., helping those who are different to become comfortable in the school community). This can be a way of introducing broader issues relating to prejudice and diversity.
- Introduce a regular time for reflection on these matters in the classroom and at home (e.g., the dinner table).

STRATEGIES THAT PROMOTE SOCIAL EMOTIONAL LEARNING

Educators can promote students' social and emotional competencies and ethical dispositions in a range of ways. In fact, we always are. As we have pointed out previously, whether we mean to or not, we are always social and emotional as well as academic teachers. Teachers explicitly and implicitly signal their values and beliefs about what matters and how they feel about students as well as about the relative importance of making mistakes, effort, strengths, and weaknesses, all of which color students' feelings about themselves. As described below, there are many ways in which we can promote students' social and emotional competencies (see Cohen, 1999, 2001, for further ideas).

Stand-Alone Courses of Study

Educators can create stand-alone courses of study to promote students' social emotional competencies. We believe that the oldest example of this is the ethics classes taught in the Ethical Culture School, an independent school in New York City founded by Felix

Adler over 100 years ago (Caroline, 1905). A more recent—and empirically studied—example can be found in New Haven, Connecticut. The Social Development Program is a K–12 curriculum-based sequence of courses mandated by every school in the city; it includes detailed lesson plans for every class (Shriver, Schwab-Stone, & DeFalco, 1999). Health education courses represent another ongoing course of study that can and, we suggest, should include ongoing social emotional educational efforts.

Some researchers have suggested that these courses may be most useful for disadvantaged youths who often grow up with dramatically less than average caring and responsive social interaction. Some youths need to learn social and emotional skills in isolation (e.g., learning what it means to assume a listening position) before they can begin to utilize these skills in a more generalized manner.

Integration of Social Emotional Education Into the Academic and Nonacademic Aspects of Class Life

Most educators do not have the time or inclination to develop a new course of study in this area. However, many, if not most, elementary and middle school teachers are quite interested in the range of ways that they can integrate social emotional learning into the life of the class in academic and nonacademic ways. There are a number of language arts, social studies, and history curricula that various organizations have developed to further linguistic (or social studies or historical) literacy as well as social emotional literacy. The Center for Social and Emotional Education works with schools and districts to support classroom teachers to infuse social emotional teaching into existing curricula.

Social emotional learning can also be integrated into the non-academic dimensions of classroom life. First, educators communicate what is most important to them in a variety of ways. To the extent that we include social and emotional goals as primary for learning, it matters. We are telling students about our values and goals. We can also integrate teaching social emotional competencies into morning meetings, into the creation of a democratic classroom, and into how we manage class and student discipline or in advisory programs.

Service Learning and Community Service

Service learning and community service provide extraordinary ways to promote students' social and emotional competences. As Fredericks (2003) has described, these efforts are overlapping. To the extent to which service learning and community service are meaningful activities for students, this is an engaging and powerful way to focus on and promote social and emotional competencies (Kaye, 2004).

Relationships

Learning is fundamentally relational: We are almost always learners in the context of the teacher-student relationship. Some of the most important emotional learning takes place in informal relations between child and teacher (Mayer & Salovey, 1997; Pianta, 1999). We suggest that it is always valuable to periodically review and reflect on what kinds of relationships we want to have and do have in school: teachers and students; educators with other educators and school staff; and educators and parents. What students see relationally is much more powerful than how we tell students to act. Our actions teach.

Teachers and administrators may influence children's ability to express and regulate emotions in two ways: directly by teaching and coaching, and indirectly by observational learning or by controlling children's exposure to different situations. Thus teachers, through their interactions with students, fellow teachers, and administrators, model for children appropriate ways to regulate emotions. Teachers also directly instruct students about how to manage and deal with distress. Earlier, we mentioned the school structure: Clearly, in the very process of designing and redesigning a comfortable learning environment, teachers and other educators construct the opportunities that children have to learn about emotion regulation (Matthews, Zeidner, & Roberts, 2002).

The Importance of Adults Walking the Talk

How invested are we—the adults working, teaching, and learning with students—in being ongoing social emotional learners ourselves? To the extent that educators and parents are active social emotional learners themselves, they provide powerful and positive role models. If teachers act rudely to one another or to school support staff, or if the teachers use a tough street style as a mechanism of control in either the classroom or the corridors, students will quickly perceive that these kinds of behaviors are tolerated in schools, and often they will act accordingly. In the vignette at the beginning of this chapter, the teacher clearly overreacted. She might have handled the whole situation with some humor, thereby giving the students a sense that she understood their reactions.

There are many reasons why most social emotional and character educational efforts fail to foster learning and behavioral change (see Cohen and Sandy, 2003, for a review). Although no systemic research has addressed this question, our work with thousands of educators, hundreds of schools, a number of state departments of education, and foreign educational ministries suggests that three major factors undermine efficacy: (1) short-term and fragmented efforts, (2) ill-conceived efforts, and (3) inadequate opportunities and support for adults to walk the talk. The importance of teachers as learners in the process of social emotional education cannot be overestimated. Discovery in relation to our colleagues, students, and constituency (parents and community) is a powerful tool to further our ability to understand, empathize, and become effective educators and role models.

SUMMARY

Teaching students the skills, knowledge, and beliefs that foster core social and emotional competencies is one of the two major strategies that creates safer and more caring schools. There is a group of core social and emotional competencies that is predictive of students' ability to learn, to solve problems in nonviolent ways, and to act in caring, related ways. Although researchers have used various labels to describe the core social and emotional competencies, the following list represents one generally agreed-upon framework for the competencies:

- Reflective and empathic abilities
- Problem-solving and decision-making abilities
- Communicative capacities
- Impulse control and anger management abilities
- Cooperative capacities
- Ability to form friendships
- Ability to recognize and appreciate diversity
- Altruistic capacities

There is a range of ways in which educators can actively promote students' social and emotional competencies:

- Through stand-alone courses of study.
- By integrating social emotional education into the existing curriculum.
- By infusing social emotional education into the nonacademic aspects of classroom life.
- Through service learning and community service.
- By example: To the extent that we are active social emotional learners, we become vital role models for our students.

It is essential that we are actively involved with being social emotional learners ourselves and that professional development activities support this goal. Social and emotional competencies should be an explicit and valued goal throughout the school. Teachers should be provided with professional development opportunities to increase their awareness of social and emotional skills. Adults and children can work collaboratively to develop a list of common values regarding rights and responsibilities within the school and make that list visible in every room.

REFLECTING ON YOUR CURRENT PRACTICE

- What are your goals?
- What can you do to clarify whether current as well as planned efforts are actually furthering your goals?
- Are students given work that is appropriate to their academic needs?
- Are there opportunities for children to excel in academic, artistic, and social domains?
- Are grouping practices flexible to help meet individual students' needs?
- Are teachers provided with professional development opportunities to help them recognize and meet the diverse needs of learners?
- Are administrators involved consistently in the teaching and learning process?
- Do teachers ask administrators for instructional assistance?
- Do teachers believe that it is important to be a reflective practitioner and to self-evaluate?
- Do teachers believe that an important part of their job is to teach social and emotional skills, knowledge, and beliefs?
- Are professional development opportunities in social and emotional learning offered to faculty and staff?
- Is social and emotional skill building a clearly articulated piece of the curriculum?
- Are teachers given ongoing administrative support in the area of social and emotional learning?
- Do adults in the school demonstrate an understanding of students' social and emotional needs?
- Do adults in the school model effective social and emotional skills?
- Do adults in the building see a relationship between their own behaviors and those of their students?
- Are students encouraged to take intellectual risks?

CHAPTER FIVE

Fostering Students' Emotional Safety for Learning

> Mary's teacher asked the class a question. Mary did not understand it. She knew the teacher had told the class many times that she really wanted to know when students were confused. But Mary felt so anxious about raising her hand that she did not do it. Mary started to become silently upset. She felt she was being silly and that she should ask her question. Even worse, she knew that her reluctance to raise her hand was getting in the way of her learning. But every time she started to, she felt this large lump of worry in her stomach and she stopped. Struggling with these experiences, Mary had a great deal of difficulty paying attention to what her fellow students and the teacher were talking about.

How safe students feel and actually are in school is a complex matter. Feeling safe and being safe are not synonymous. There is an interactive set of societal, community, school climate, relational, and internal factors that contribute both to the feeling of safety and to how safe students actually are in school. In this chapter, we focus on the experience of emotional safety and what fosters this optimal psychological foundation for learning. In the vignette above, for example, Mary did not feel emotionally safe enough to ask a question in class.

How do you feel right now as you are reading these words? As you pay attention to your experience, including how safe or anxious you are feeling right now, you are reflecting on what we refer to as the experience of emotional safety. We suggest that the experience of emotional safety refers to feeling safe enough with our own internal feelings, thoughts, and impulses. Feeling emotionally safe allows learners to take healthy risks, to not know, and to be confused. When students feel safe emotionally, they are most able to be active learners.

Remember for a moment when you were a child in class. When did you feel safe to make mistakes and to let others know that you were confused? When did you believe—rightly or wrongly—that you needed to hide these experiences from others? Most of us remember moments when we anxiously feared that we would be embarrassed and humiliated if we allowed others to see us being confused or not knowing. As adults, it is so obvious that being open about not knowing allows us to learn.

PROMOTING EMOTIONAL SAFETY

There is a range of steps we can take to foster students' sense of emotional safety. In fact, everything we have detailed in the two preceding chapters that focused on systemic school climate issues as well as on how we can promote students' social and emotional competency is directly relevant to fostering a greater sense of emotional safety. Certain social emotional competencies contribute importantly to the development of emotional safety: impulse control, reflective capacities, and empathic abilities—being able to recognize that others struggle, that it is okay and normal to struggle.

A safe and caring school climate clearly creates an optimal climate for learning in general. Students (and faculty), for example, do not feel safe when they see violence on a regular basis (Overstreet & Braun, 2000). The amount of drug and alcohol abuse present also colors how safe students feel (Reese et al., 2001; Willson et al., 2000). Having friends and being helpful contribute to a sense of safety and success (Cabrera et al., 2000).

Although we are not aware of any classroom-based studies, it is clear that how the teacher develops rules and how students treat one another importantly influence how students treat themselves. They will internalize the treatment they receive in the classroom. For example, if students are allowed to belittle one another for making a mistake, it will increase the likelihood that students will belittle themselves.

Certainly, individual factors will also color how safe a student feels in school. For example, if a student's parents are fighting or on the verge of divorce, the student will naturally feel less safe. Students who are struggling with any number of disorders (e.g., severe anxiety or depression) will naturally feel less safe and more out of control.

What follows are strategies that educators and school-based mental health professionals have found useful to further students' sense of emotional safety.

Creating a Caring Classroom

There are steps teachers can take to create a caring classroom that explicitly values caring and healthy risk taking (e.g., letting others know that we do not know or are confused about a given issue). For example, when a teacher has a dialogue with the students at the beginning of the year about what kind of classroom the children want to have, most want to have fun and feel safe. Occasionally, students also give voice to wanting to learn. In any case, this dialogue creates a platform for talking about what kinds of rules are needed to feel safe in the classroom. Although the teacher is naturally in charge, collaborative discussions along these lines typically allow the teacher to incorporate students' suggestions for classroom-based rules that further social and emotional safety. These discussions and the creation of what some call a democratic classroom foster a sense of co-ownership in classroom life as well as clarity about what is and is not allowed. Watson and Ecken (2003) have written wonderful and clear guides that can support teachers doing just this. The more teachers create a classroom that is well managed, forbid teasing and ridicule, and rejoice when students take healthy risks (e.g., not knowing), the more students will feel a sense of trust and emotional security.

Acting as a Role Model

Adults are always role models for students, intentionally or not, for good or bad. In what ways do you demonstrate that it is okay (and even important) to make mistakes and to be confused in class? Often adults shield children from these moments. When we show that we are not always understandable and that this is normal, it can importantly foster students' acceptance of these moments as well.

It is useful to explicitly and repeatedly tell students that you welcome their questions and the experience of not knowing. Also, it is very useful to let students know about moments that we may have, in and out of class, when we do not know everything. Elementary and middle school students are particularly likely to imagine that adults are usually, if not always, knowledgeable, in control, and clear about the right thing to do next. (As we all know, this idea tends to fade in adolescence.)

Showing Appreciation and Reinforcement

What do you appreciate and reinforce in the classroom? We all attempt to maintain a balance between the process of learning and the outcome or final product (e.g., the final test scores for a semester project). To the extent that we explicitly recognize and appreciate students allowing themselves to take healthy risks in class, we are reinforcing the importance of this fundamental process.

Relating the Climate of the Classroom and the School

If we are working to create a safe and caring classroom where students feel safe to make mistakes, optimally the principal and our fellow teachers are working to create a schoolwide culture that echoes these same goals. As we describe in Chapters 3 and 8, there is a variety of steps we can take together to make the school safer and more caring, participatory, and responsive—a safe place where people can tell the truth.

SUMMARY

Emotional safety refers to accepting and feeling safe enough with our own internal feelings, thoughts, and impulses. Feeling safe emotionally provides the foundation for healthy risk taking as well as for learners to be able to openly not know and be confused. It is normal that children often feel embarrassed about not knowing, being confused, and a variety of other experiences that contribute to feeling not fully in control. Feeling emotionally safe creates a platform for discovery and learning. Optimally, the climate of the school echoes the climate of the classroom. For example, both the principal and the classroom teacher focus intermittently on the importance of trusting and caring relationships.

REFLECTING ON YOUR CURRENT PRACTICE

- How important do I think it really is for students to feel emotionally safe?
- When I was a child, what was the most important experience or experiences in school that fostered my emotional safety as a learner? What were the most important experiences that made me feel unsafe?
- What do I do now as an educator to foster students' emotional safety in my class?
- What do I do now as an educator to foster students' emotional safety in school?
- What do you think are some of the major factors that contribute to students feeling emotionally unsafe?
- To what extent do I explicitly talk about the importance of being able to not know and be confused? How do I actually reinforce this with my students?
- Do I have a formal or informal class policy about how it is okay or not okay for students to react to one another (e.g., laughing at mistakes)?
- To what extent is this issue discussed in department meetings, faculty meetings, and professional develop-

ment forums? So often, physical and social safety issues (e.g., bullying) are so problematic in school that we rarely focus on creating the internal climate for learning.

- To what extent do my goals for creating a caring classroom echo the school's goals for creating a caring school?

CHAPTER SIX

Bullying: The Triangle of Bully, Victim, and Bystander

You are the assistant principal in a large high school. One of your more experienced counselors tells you that she would like to talk with you about one of her students. She begins by saying, "Harold is making marked improvement in his studies but only God knows how he's doing in his personal life. After Halloween, Harold didn't come to school for a whole week. When he finally came in, he said that he's been having difficulty concentrating on school. When I asked why, he said that he and his only two friends, two older boys who come from his native country, were hanging out together after school the previous week before going to work at a restaurant. One of the boys started joking that they were going to rape Harold and started bullying him to drop his pants. Then they pulled him into an alley and one boy pulled his pants down while the other one pinned him on the ground on his stomach. Harold began to yell for help and the two boys shushed him. Things got intensely frightening for Harold." She says Harold said to her, "I knew I had to do something to escape, so with all my strength I hit the boy who had pinned me down, freed one foot, and kicked as hard as I could the crotch of the other. I don't know how I wiggled free, but then I got up and ran. When I got home, I told my brother that I don't want to work with them anymore and that I don't want them as friends. Without even asking why, he belted me hard, first on the face and then in the stomach. But I won't go back there to work ever. They're not my friends; they're faggots." The guidance counselor says that she felt weak after hearing the story and would like to talk over what happened and how she should handle the case.

In the previous chapters, we indicated that social and emotional education is characterized by respect and consideration for oneself and others. But what happens when social and emotional learning breaks down? When an incident of bullying occurs, the ideal of a school as a place of learning is ruptured. As we have pointed out, schools inevitably teach morality—intentionally or not. Kids are constantly picking up adult signals. Children and youth learn both through direct instruction and through a kind of osmosis, observing what kinds of behaviors the adults tolerate. For a very long time, bullying was tolerated and was common in schools throughout Western society. Today, attitudes are changing, and bullying is no longer accepted as a normal facet of child and adolescent development. In this chapter, we attempt to understand bullying itself and examine some accepted definitions of bullying. We study the impact of bullying on the individual and the school, as well as some schoolwide prevention methods.

We begin this chapter with a new assumption, that all successful antibullying programs start with this principle: "In this school, bullying is not tolerated. Here there is no such thing as an outsider or a passive bystander." When bullying occurs, there is virtually always a witness. One of the essential questions that this chapter addresses is how members of the school community can develop the skills and dispositions that support "upstander" behavior rather than passive bystander behavior.

After the tragic incident at Columbine High School in Littleton, Colorado, the U.S. Secret Service published a report on a study that examined 37 school-related shootings that had occurred during the previous two decades. The researchers wanted to get the shooters' own perspectives on their decision to engage in a school-based attack. In over two thirds of the cases, students who attacked their classmates or teachers (in almost all of the incidents with handguns, rifles, or shotguns) had been bullied by others prior to the incident. In many of these cases, the bullying was long-standing and no one in the school had done anything to forestall it. What is also startling in this study is the fact that in over

75% of the incidents, other students knew that the attack was going to take place before it occurred. Yet none of these teenagers felt comfortable or close enough to a faculty member in the school to reveal what they knew even when they knew exactly what the attacker planned to do (U.S. Secret Service Safe School Initiative, 2000).

Professor Dan Olweus of the University of Bergen in Norway was the pioneer in research on the phenomenon of bullying. He was able to persuade the educational authorities in Norway of the importance of stopping bullying in schools, and with their cooperation he mounted a national campaign aimed at its systematic reduction. Two years later, evaluation studies showed a reduction of bullying in Bergen schools by a remarkable 50% (Rigby, 1996). Olweus's studies inspired a whole generation of researchers and educators to ask themselves why we, as a society, have been so tolerant of bullying.

Spurred on by Olweus's studies, researchers throughout Europe, Australia, Japan, and, somewhat later, here in the United States began to study bullying and, more importantly, began to believe that something could be done to curtail it. Thus the revolution in our thinking about bullying in schools began in Scandinavia in the early 1970s and continues today throughout the world (Rigby, 1996). This chapter addresses the question of what we have learned about bullying and what we can do to better prevent it from occurring in our schools, communities, and homes.

EXAMINING BULLYING

The phenomenon of bullying has received a great deal of attention in recent years in the media—in sensational magazine articles and the daily press, as well as educational journals, not to mention on the Internet. Awareness that bullying can be combated is gradually seeping into the public consciousness. Just type the word *bul-*

lying into your search engine and you will be treated to about 23 million Web sites offering advice, personal assistance, and anti-bullying programs.

What Is Bullying?

There is some controversy about exactly what we mean when we use the term *bullying*. Some writers see bullying behavior as a subset of the more inclusive term *school violence*. For them, violence refers strictly to physical force or power. It does not include verbal aggression, relational aggression such as rumor telling, or social exclusion (Smith, 2002). But the World Health Organization uses a broader definition of school violence that includes bullying: "The intentional use of physical and psychological force or power, threatened or actual, against oneself, another person, or against a group or community, that either results in or has a high likelihood of resulting in injury, death, psychological harm, mal-development, or deprivation" (see www.health.fi/connect, cited in Smith, 2002, p. 5). Other writers use a still broader definition that includes institutional violence or structural violence, which is the equivalent of social injustice and, in terms of our discussion in this book, would include situations in which our society does not provide adequate schooling or health facilities for children.

In this book, we use a definition of school bullying that derives from Olweus's original work and that most researchers would agree with: Bullying is the repeated (not just once) harming of another through words or physical attack on the school grounds or on the way to or from school. The act of bullying is unfair, because the bully is either stronger or more verbally or socially skilled than the victim(s). An individual or group may carry these actions out (Hazler, Miller, Carney, & Green, 2001).

Thus, according to our definition, bullying may be psychological or physical, or both. Note also that an individual or a group may carry out these actions. The bully may be a student (male or female) or an adult. Bullying is characterized by repetitiveness and an unbalanced relationship—one person has more power than the other. Bullying may take on less direct forms—like gossiping, spreading rumors, and shunning and social exclusion. Teasing or giving nicknames to a person can also be a form of bullying that can be extremely oppressive emotionally. A wide variety of negative behaviors fall under the umbrella term of bullying: name calling, inappropriate gestures, physical abuse, threatening, taunting, spitting, stealing, shoving, kicking, carrying a weapon, extortion, spreading false rumors, and social exclusion. Emotional and social forms of bullying can be just as devastating as the cruder physical forms. The effects can last a lifetime (Chapell, in press; Hugh-Jones & Smith, 1999).

Bullying and social exclusion in schools can overlap in complicated ways. As we have discussed, bullying refers to the repeated harming of another through words or physical attack on the school grounds or on the way to or from school. Bullying is unfair, because the bully is either stronger or more verbally or socially skilled than the victim. When students form a group and exclude others, purposely or not, it can certainly feel like bullying. And it may be, or it may not. Sometimes groups of middle school students, for example, are just great friends who are not purposely excluding others. This is one of the many important topics that we suggest teachers, health educators, and other raise when they talk about bully-victim-witness behavior in school.

How Prevalent Is Bullying?

Ideally, school should be a sanctuary where students feel safe—a place where parents can send their children in the morning and not have to worry about violence. Our own work in middle schools and high schools has led us to believe that many school staff and parents underestimate the prevalence of bullying, while students consistently report widespread bullying. At some schools, teachers will claim that "we do not have real bullying here, just a lot of teasing." Such attitudes minimize the harmful effects of teasing, which can have serious and even devastating emotional side effects.

In a survey of more than 15,000 sixth through tenth graders at public and private schools in the United States, "30 percent of the students reported bullying others, being the target of bullying, or both" (Bowman, 2001). In a study of fourth through eighth graders, about 15% reported being severely distressed by bullying and 22% reported academic difficulties stemming from mistreatment by peers (Hoover & Oliver, 1996). In general, about one in four children are bullied and approximately 282,000 students are attacked in secondary schools every month (Schmitt, 1999, cited in ERIC, 2001). Many studies have shown a decline in bullying as grade levels increase from 6th grade through 12th grade (Lumsden, 2002).

Students are not the only bullies in schools. Although the focus of this chapter is student bullying, in our work with schools across America we commonly discover that bullying is a serious adult problem as well. Parents bully teachers. Teachers bully parents, colleagues, and sometimes students. Administrators bully teachers. The issue of adult bullying in schools is only beginning to be acknowledged and studied. A study of educators, for example, showed that teachers who experienced bullying themselves when young are more likely to both bully students and experience bullying by students both in and outside the classroom (Twemlow, Fonagy, Sacco, & Brethour, 2006). We have often worked in schools where it is clear that until we address these very charged adult issues, we will not be able to work with student bullying.

What Is the Impact of Bullying?

In the vignette at the beginning of this chapter, it appears at first that there are no bystanders: the two older boys drag the victim into an alley in order to commit their awful crime. But when the victim, Harold, confides in the guidance counselor, she becomes a witness to the violent action. This exposure to violence always has its effects. The counselor said that she felt weak and that she wanted to talk the matter over with her supervisor. That was her reaction to the incident, and it is important to note that witnessing violence, even secondhand, even at a week's distance in the quiet of a counseling office, exposes us to the way others have been violated and has its effects on us. Observing our own reactions to being exposed to violence helps us understand what we can do to help others heal when they have been subjected to violence.

Bullying can have a profound impact on youths, short term and long term. Students who are targeted by bullies often have difficulty concentrating on their schoolwork, and their academic performance tends to be marginal to poor (Ballard, 1999). Typically, bullied students feel anxious, and this anxiety may in turn produce a variety of physical and emotional ailments (Lumsden, 2002). Bullying affects school performance and attendance in a number of ways: Some students stay home for fear of further harassment; some try to avoid certain places within the school where bullying takes place; some hide in teachers' offices; some ask for transfers to other schools; some drop out of school altogether. Students who are members of various minority groups (e.g., racial, sexual orientation) are often targets for bullying. Gay students report that they are constantly harassed. This is particularly tragic for boys and girls who are still unsure about their sexual orientation and who may become the butt of jokes. Gay students who are surer of their own sexuality have it no easier if the school does not question the macho-man jock culture or traditional roles for females. For administrators, one way of dealing with bullying is not dealing with it. Anthropologists call this avoidance behavior. It happens in schools when teachers put on blinders—when they see bullying taking place yet refuse to deal with it.

WITNESSING BULLYING IN SCHOOLS

As we have pointed out, bullying is more than a dyadic relationship, a two-person affair between a bully (or group of bullies) and a victim. In fact, the phenomenon of bullying is almost always a triadic relationship involving three parties—the victim, the bully, and a bystander (or bystanders). Many studies have taken note of the importance of the bystander's role in understanding bullying (Slaby et al., 1994; Twemlow, 1999).

It is extremely important to understand the bystander role if we are going to fully appreciate the phenomenon of bullying. The bystander may be a child or an adult. The bystander may play an active or a passive role. The bystander may identify with the victim or with the bully (Twemlow, 1999). The bystander may or may not have an obligation to intervene to stop the bullying. Bystanders may have various motives for standing by—mere curiosity, or an attempt to learn how to defend themselves should the bully turn on them next.

In the above vignette, what about Harold's brother, who hit him when he came home and recounted the incident? He, too, was a witness to the violence, but one who for his own reasons identified with the bullies rather than with Harold, thereby increasing Harold's trauma instead of helping to ameliorate it, as perhaps Harold had expected. So Harold was doubly traumatized, once on the street and again at home.

Another example might serve to illustrate what we mean by *passive bystander*. One of us (JD) operated a tutoring program at a large, overcrowded high school in which university students served as tutors for ninth grade students who were at risk of dropping out of school. One day, in the hallway right outside the tutoring room, a fierce fight broke out during lunch period as one older student attacked a recent immigrant. As the two pummeled each other with their fists and dragged one another across the corridor floor, a large crowd of students gathered and formed a tight knot around the two combatants. The university students, interrupted in their tutoring by the loud commotion, came out and noticed that the security guard who was usually present at that spot was missing. So one of the university students took matters into his own hands and plowed through the knot of onlookers and separated the two students, thus ending the incident.

This little episode has many facets. The university student went beyond his role of outside tutor in separating the two students. The security guard came up the stairs too late to do anything. Some observers said that the guard had deliberately avoided the confrontation. The adults dispersed the crowd back to their classrooms, and the incident was over.

We relate this story here to illustrate the complex nature of the bullying phenomenon. The university student who intervened (even though he was not supposed to) was an upstander who acted to prevent the two fighting students from harming one another. The security guard who avoided coming up to the corridor even though he knew a fight was in progress was derelict in his duty and indeed was a passive bystander. Inside the knot of students watching the aggression, some of the bystanders might have been cheering for the bully, others for the victim: the roles of bully, victim, and bystander are all interchangeable and can shift with lightning speed. One might even question whether this was a bullying incident. Perhaps it was just a fight between two students. Nevertheless, the same principles for preventing school violence apply.

MYTHS AND REALITIES ABOUT BULLYING

People in the United States have been slowly becoming aware of the toxic effects of bullying. Nevertheless, numerous myths about bullying persist. Here are a few of the more common myths you might hear both inside and outside schools:

- Bullying will always be with us—there is nothing we can do about it.
- Bullies are tough or mean kids who will not change.
- Victims need to toughen up and not be so sensitive.
- Dealing with bullying is not in my job description.
- Girls rarely bully.
- It's just a little teasing, for God's sake.
- It's part of the culture. You'll never change it.
- What do you expect from some unruly teenagers?
- There are some forms of bullying that are impossible to eradicate.

- Boys need some taunting to toughen them up. It builds character.
- What harm can a little bullying be?

The reality is that bullying should not be considered as a harmless and normal stage of child socialization. Many schools both here and abroad have initiated antibullying campaigns that have had a major impact on reducing school bullying. We can do something about bullying. Any awareness campaign begins with the realization that we should not tolerate bullying in our schools. Bullying is no more acceptable than other social ills we have begun to condemn in our society such as driving while intoxicated or domestic abuse.

Students do indeed engage in mean behavior toward other kids, and they sometimes present themselves as having a tough demeanor. But that does not mean that there is not another side of their personality that is susceptible to invitations from a caring, nonjudgmental adult who takes an interest in their welfare.

"Victims need to toughen up and not be so sensitive." The truth of the matter is that victims are truly being subjected to constant harassment by bullies and that often it is only responsible adults who can correct the situation. This compassion means taking the victimization seriously and intervening to stop the bullying. It also means dealing directly with the emotional issues of both bullies and victims.

"Dealing with bullying is not in my job description." In fact, we are all potential witnesses and we all make conscious or unrecognized choices to be passive bystanders (and hence, collude with the problem) or upstanders.

Girls are not above being bullies. They may also be involved in more serious behaviors like carrying weapons.

Teasing, name calling, and provocative taunting can be a particularly vicious form of bullying and should not be treated lightly. The victims can suffer lifelong consequences.

There is no evidence that bullying builds character or that it fosters camaraderie, as is sometimes alleged. Programs that pro-

mote mutual respect and understanding of one another's differences are effective in building character.

WAYS OF COPING WITH BULLYING

Many books and articles have been written on ways to prevent
bullying. In the earlier literature, research focused on attempting
to understand the characteristics of bullies or victims (e.g., Farrington, 1993). In this older model, it was as if there were only two
characters in the bullying scenario: the bully (the perpetrator) and
the victim. Gradually, scholars began to become aware of the sim-
plicity of this dualistic theory. They realized that there was a third
character missing in their analyses, namely, the bystander. With
the entry of the bystander (also often referred to as the witness) a
paradigm shift began to take place in bullying studies, shifting
away from a simple two-dimensional model (bully–victim) to a
three-dimensional one encompassing the bully, the victim, and
the bystander.

We believe that it is important, therefore, to begin by raising
the consciousness of the entire school community to the serious-
ness of bullying and its consequences. Successful antibullying programs, like the Olweus Bullying Prevention program, operate at
three levels: (1) schoolwide interventions, (2) classroom interventions, and (3) individual interventions.

Schoolwide interventions consist of a campaign to raise
awareness of the problem as well as to reflectively talk about what
kind of school community everyone wants to have; forming a bullying prevention committee; taking a survey of bullying problems
in the schools; training for committee members and staff; increasing supervision; and adoption of schoolwide rules against bullying (Twemlow, Fonagy, & Sacco, 2002). As we detail below, this
schoolwide effort needs to include an examination of the role of
the witness. In schools, there is virtually always a witness, directly
or indirectly, to moments of bullying and victimization. Students
and adults alike make decisions either to be passive bystanders or

to be upstanders: to act in ways that say no to bully-victim behavior. Schoolwide interventions also need to include ways to recognize and honor upstander behavior.

Classroom interventions involve setting up classroom rules against bullying, holding regular class meetings to discuss bullying issues at school, and holding informational meetings with all the parents. Classroom interventions are also where we can and need to provide students with an opportunity to practice being upstanders. Individual-level components include interventions with children who chronically act as a bully or a victim and interventions with children who are bullied. It is essential that educators, school-based mental health professionals, and parents act as a team to accomplish these individual-level goals (Cohen, 2006).

In this section, we outline a series of research-based goals and steps that other schools have found useful in coping with bullying. First, we outline a schoolwide process of setting in motion a school and community discussion to develop a shared vision about safety. Second, we describe how it is useful to develop scripts that support upstander behavior and to create opportunities to practice being an upstander. Third, we describe the importance of recognizing and working with at-risk and troubled students who often become chronic bullies or victims. Finally, we underscore the importance of reinforcing upstander behavior through academic and nonacademic aspects of school life.

Conducting a Schoolwide Discussion About the Bully, Victim, and Witness

When was the last time you initiated a schoolwide discussion with your faculty, students, and parents about the kind of school people want? This is an important discussion to consider planning. It can set in motion a community-wide discussion about what people need to do so that students feel safe in school. In fact, virtually no one wants to be teased, bullied, or hurt. (There are rare instances when people do want to be hurt, and this signifies a serious problem.) Our experience suggests that most people hope that if they are being hurt, someone will help them. In any case, this discussion creates the platform for teachers and school leaders to introduce the notion of the witness, as explained earlier.

- What would make it more or less likely that you could have this kind of discussion in your school?
- What kind of training and support do you think your staff—or you—might need to conduct this kind of discussion?
- What could derail this discussion?

Parents play an essential role here too. They are essential partners in any successful antibullying campaign. Research shows that the success of any program is 60% grounded in whether the same kinds of approaches are used at home (Pollack, 1996). Sometimes parents need to be educated. Some schools have organized support groups for parents who are having problems supervising their teenagers. This kind of emotional support can be most helpful for single parents who have experienced domestic violence or when the youth has bullied or even assaulted the parent.

Developing Scripts and Practice That Support Upstander Behavior

An important component of an antibullying effort is to develop a series of scripts that support upstander behavior. At the Center for Social and Emotional Education, we have found that it is most useful for each school to develop its own set of scripts. In this way, students and staff are coauthors of this work. There can be a range of scripts:

- Very direct verbal confrontational communications— "You are being a bully. We have talked about how this is not okay in our school. I wish you would stop this now."
- Direct but less confrontational communications—"I am really uncomfortable with how you are talking to this

person. This does not feel okay to me. We have talked about this in class."
- Indirect but nonetheless upstander behavior that occurs when a student is too frightened to directly address bully-victim behavior—a procedure that supports students going to specified adults in the school building to report what is going on.

Practice, practice, and more practice is an essential process that promotes learning and changes behavior. Being an upstander is anxiety provoking. We cannot know how the bully or the victim will react. To promote caring and responsible school communities necessarily involves sustained practice and positive reinforcement. Just as we ensure that all people within a school understand the dangers of a fire and practice what to do when there may be a fire, we need to do the same with bully-victim behavior.

Research shows that students need to be able to practice being an upstander three to four times a week. This does not need to last more than 5 or 10 minutes. At the end of a class or in an advisory period (an "advisory" is a recent term used in school to denote a period during which the teacher can give individual attention to the student for academics or personal issues), the following steps provide an authentic and engaging opportunity to reflect and practice being an upstander:

1. The teacher asks if one or two students can report a moment when they saw some form of bully-victim behavior.
2. They are asked to create a mini role-play situation where other students enact the roles of bully, victim, and witness. It is essential that the teacher give students implicit or explicit permission to describe whatever happened: bystander or upstander behavior. This is enacted.
3. Students are then asked how they might have man-

aged this situation differently. This is then done in a role-play. The teacher needs to ask students to explain what was easy or not so easy about this.
4. Upstander behavior is celebrated.

Developing and practicing scripts furthers several goals:

- Students can develop social emotional skills.
- This fundamental question or theme becomes an ongoing topic in the minds and hearts of students.
- Teachers can empathically recognize, support, and reinforce upstander behavior.

Recognizing At-Risk and Troubled Students

Students who chronically bully and those who chronically fall into the role of victim are often signaling that they have psychological or psychiatric problems. When we see chronic bully or victim behavior, educators, parents, and mental health professionals need to work together to understand and address these behaviors. It is not uncommon, for example, that students who chronically bully at school are bullied within their own homes and neighborhoods. Often, this school behavior signals complicated problems that teachers cannot address alone. Educators and mental health professionals need to work as partners.

Reinforcing Upstander Behavior

Reinforcement shapes behavior. There are two important ways that school leaders can powerfully reinforce upstander behavior: (1) through infusing this theme into language arts and social studies, and (2) by recognizing and honoring upstander behavior.

Infusing awareness in language arts and social studies. If language arts and social studies teachers choose to, it is relatively easy to infuse these themes into academic study. Teachers can ask students to consider whether anyone is being a bully or a victim in a given novel or period of history. Through reflection, essay writing, and role playing, these literary and historical moments provide rich opportunity for teachers and students to consider what contributed to the bully-victim behavior and how others acted and reacted: as bystanders or upstanders. This focus can also be easily applied to many current social situations. In your neighborhood, for example, who (if anyone) is a chronic bully or victim?

Several existing curricula focus on just these issues. *Facing History and Ourselves* (Storm, 1994) is a social studies curriculum guide that initially focused on the Holocaust as an area of study. In recent years, they have added important resources about periods of time that were colored and shaped by prejudice, extraordinary bullying behavior, and, to a greater or lesser extent, passive bystander behavior (e.g., the American civil rights movement, recent events in Rwanda). The 4R's Program (reading, writing, respect, and resolution) is a language arts curriculum that has a similar but somewhat wider focus (Phillips & Roderick, 2001). The Center for Social and Emotional Education has also developed a series of professional development resources to support teachers infusing social, emotional, and ethical goals and linked pedagogical methods into existing language arts and social studies curricula.

Recognizing and honoring upstander behavior. What do we recognize and honor in school? Too often, we only talk about problems. It is well known that carrots are much more powerful than sticks. Emerging research indicates that periodically recognizing and honoring upstander behavior is an important component of this effort. In addition to recognizing upstander behavior in the context of ongoing classroom-based practice as noted above, upstander behavior can be honored in many ways. Some schools, for example, ask students to write about a fellow student who acted as a silent hero or was an upstander. These notes are put in boxes and periodically collected by the principal. Periodically, these students are recognized for being silent heroes. This is one of many ways that we can catch (or recognize) students being helpful and caring to fellow members of the school community. It is very important to remember, however, that positive rewards alone have a limited impact on school climate and can even backfire. The bully-victim-witness framework has the potential not only to significantly reduce bullying but to substantively promote caring, responsible, and democratic school communities. Our goal is to support students' intrinsic inclination to act as upstanders. Depending on how recognition and positive rewards are given in schools, students can find themselves doing good only to get an external reward, and other students who do not get the prize will end up feeling dispirited.

SUMMARY

Over the last decade, there has been growing awareness that bullying and bully-victim behavior are serious and pervasive problems that complicate K–12 students' ability to learn and develop in healthy ways. In fact, they are among the most common social problems that prevent students from feeling safe in schools. Within the context of schoolwide, classroom, and individual considerations, we have suggested that it is essential that we expand our thinking about bully-victim behavior to include the witness. When people bully, there is virtually always someone else who sees, hears, or learns about it: There are witnesses. So often, students and adults alike fall into the role of passive bystander: We see bully-victim behavior and do nothing. Passive bystanders collude with bully-victim behavior and implicitly communicate that this behavior is okay.

We have outlined a series of steps that school leaders need to consider systemically, instructionally, and individually. On a schoolwide basis, it is essential that school leaders communicate that bullying is unacceptable. Although there is no single best way to communicate this, we have outlined a series of steps that school leaders can consider to set in motion a discussion about the kind of school people want. Students, like all of us, want and need to feel safe. Naturally, this leads to questions about how we want others to act if we are in trouble, passive bystanders, and upstanders. But raising awareness is not enough. Students need to learn strategies and scripts that they can use when they see bullying. They need to be able to practice being upstanders. This instructional level is key. It is also important that school leaders consider how they will recognize and reinforce upstander behavior. Schoolwide strategies that recognize and reinforce upstander behavior send a powerful message to the school community: We care about and value upstander behavior.

When schools adopt a bully-victim-bystander/upstander campaign, we are not just reducing social violence. We are also setting in motion a process of social justice and democratic education. What kind of school community do we want? How do we want to treat one another? How do we ensure that no one in our community is abused? These are questions that touch on our vision for democratic communities. Promoting upstander behavior also promotes some of the essential skills and dispositions that provide the foundation for participation in a democracy (Cohen & Michelli, 2006).

REFLECTING ON YOUR CURRENT PRACTICE

- How prevalent is bullying in your school community? Student bullying? Adult bullying? Very importantly, how do you know this?
- How does your school currently recognize and address bully behavior?
- To what extent is there a schoolwide commitment to not tolerating bullying and to the notion that we must

all actively stand up to bully-victim behavior as opposed to inadvertently falling into a passive bystander
role?
- What are you doing at schoolwide, instructional (teaching skills that will reduce bully-victim behavior), and
individual (educator, parent, mental health professional partnership) levels? What is most and least effective about these efforts?

CHAPTER SEVEN

Recognizing and Assisting Traumatized Children

with Roy Lubit

Cathy was a typical 12-year-old girl. She was a bit above average as a student. She had several friends, participated in her school chorus, and was oppositional at times, but was doing pretty well. Her parents were educated, hard working, and concerned. Her new stepfather gave her more attention than her father had, and she seemed to like it.

Around her 13th birthday, she seemed to go into a bit of a slump. She was moodier than she had been. She stayed to herself more and often left the house. When her parents asked about it, she brushed off their questions. They did not want to be intrusive and dropped the issue. They assumed that since the teachers had not told them of any problems, things were basically fine. Her teachers, after all, spent much more time with her than they did. Her parents assumed it was just a stage. At school, her teachers also noticed that she was quieter than usual. They were preoccupied with teaching and the students who disrupted the classroom. They assumed that Cathy's parents would take care of any problems. Her pediatrician noticed she was ill at ease when she saw him. He asked Cathy if everything was okay. Cathy said yes, and the pediatrician said no more.

Things were not okay. Cathy was being sexually abused by her new stepbrother, Alex. She did not know what to say. Alex said he would just deny it if she said anything. Cathy did not want to wreck her Mom's new marriage. She had also been told to stop complaining when she had first started saying that

she did not like Alex. Her parents, teachers, and pediatrician
did not speak together. If they had, they might have realized
the magnitude of the change in her.

Emotional trauma from physical or emotional abuse, or experiencing situations in which one's safety is in serious jeopardy, affects a
significant percentage of our children. Researchers estimate that
over 6.1 million children between the ages of 10 and 16 have suffered some sort of traumatic event that places them at risk for problems with relationships and school. These events include being
physically or sexually abused, being exposed to domestic violence,
experiencing a disaster or serious car accident, witnessing or suffering violence in the community, or suffering serious bullying. Many
additional children are subjected to other traumatic events such as
divorce or relocation that overwhelm their abilities to cope.

Trauma interferes with children's ability to learn. Moreover,
traumatized children often disrupt the classroom, interfering with
everyone else's ability to learn. Knowing how to recognize, support, and refer traumatized children will both foster the ability of
the traumatized student to learn and improve the atmosphere of
the entire class. It will also help to free teachers from dealing with
discipline problems and allow them to return to teaching academic skills.

SOURCES OF TRAUMA

We divide sources of trauma into three categories: single-incident
trauma, chronic trauma, and high-stress trauma. The symptoms
of individuals in the different groups overlap but also have significant differences.

Single-Incident Trauma

Single-incident traumas include being in a car accident, experiencing a natural or manmade disaster, or being the victim of an as-

sault, all of which can lead to post-traumatic stress disorder (PTSD). The definition mental health professionals use for PTSD requires the individual to have experienced intense fear, helplessness, or horror in response to exposure to a serious traumatic event that caused or threatened serious harm or violation of bodily integrity. The word *exposure* is used because one can develop PTSD from witnessing others being hurt or hearing about the traumatic event of a loved one. Roughly 150,000 children under age 18, including 50,000 children under age 12, suffer rape, attempted rape, or sexual assault each year in the United States (U.S. Department of Justice, 1997, 2000). Over 200,000 children age 14 years and under are injured in car accidents each year. Far more are injured if you add those between the ages of 15 and 18. One third of children in significant car accidents develop PTSD.

Chronic Trauma

Disorders of extreme stress, termed chronic trauma, also affect hundreds of thousands of children. Three million children per year are referred to child protective services for abuse or serious neglect. One third of the cases are substantiated, and half of these (half a million) are so severe that the children are removed from their homes (Malik, 2002; National Center on Child Abuse and Neglect, 1997). Estimates of the number of children who witness domestic violence run from 3 to 10 million (Edleson, 1999; Straus, Gelles, & Steinmetz, 2006). In one survey, from grades 9 to 12, 12% of girls and 5% of boys said that they had been sexually abused (Commonwealth Fund Survey of the Health of Adolescent Girls, 1997). Community violence is a particularly serious problem in the inner cities. Fitzpatrick and Boldizar (1993), studying low-income African American youths aged 7 to 18 attending a federally funded summer camp program, found that more than 70% of the children and adolescents reported being victims of at least one violent act, close to 85% had witnessed at least one violent act, and 43% had witnessed a murder. Far more heard gunshots and heard about murders.

Prior to 9/11, 64% of New York City public school children in grades 4 to 12 had been exposed to a traumatic event, including seeing someone killed or seriously injured, or seeing the violent or accidental death of a close friend or family member (Hoven, 2005). Even more would do so by the end of their time in school. Large numbers of children have left their homes and lived in shelters for a period.

Bullying also takes an enormous toll. As explained in Chapter 6, bullying differs from age-typical quarreling or teasing by being prolonged, one-sided, and intending harm. It can be physical (hitting, kicking, robbing, pushing, unwanted sexual touching), verbal (insulting, threatening, taunting), or psychological torture (extortion, intimidation, spreading rumors, excluding). Bullying hurts both perpetrators and victims.

Perpetrators fail to learn appropriate inhibitions against hurting others and instead receive gratification for being abusive. Victims often have problems learning in school, become depressed, may become isolated, suffer fear and anxiety, suffer humiliation and diminution of self-esteem, fear going to school, engage in substance abuse, and may develop PTSD or turn to violence themselves. Those who simply watch bullying probably also suffer negative effects.

High-Stress Trauma

A third group of children are subject to parental illness, divorce, or other stressful home situations that lead to significant levels of anxiety or depression and impair their ability to concentrate and cooperate.

Traumatic events have a wide-ranging impact. In the vignette opening this chapter, Cathy not only became depressed and withdrew from friends and school, but her self-image and core identity suffered. She began experiencing herself as tainted, vulnerable, and weak. She was filled with a sense of guilt. In addition, her withdrawal and poor concentration prevented her from continuing to learn age-appropriate skills. Falling behind academically and socially further damaged her self-esteem and core identity. Even if the trauma of abuse was somehow suddenly resolved, having fallen behind socially and academically would present difficult hurdles to overcome given her lowered self-esteem and core identity as only a mediocre student and social individual. In addition, her future ability to enjoy sex was markedly damaged, as was her ability to protect herself from sexual predators.

Being subjected or exposed to serious injury or violation of bodily integrity can set off a series of destructive psychological and neurophysiological processes. People find themselves experiencing painful memories of the event, especially when faced with reminders. The resulting distress impairs their academic and social performance. Some children become anxious and withdraw, while others become agitated and disrupt others' activities. Children tend to play and replay the event in an attempt to gain mastery. Meanwhile, in an attempt to blunt their pain, victims often become numb and withdraw from other people and their usual activities. This withdrawal and loss of interest impairs functioning and the ability to learn new skills needed to succeed in the future. Hyperarousal is also an important result. The tendency to strong startle reactions, poor concentration, and being continually on edge also impairs functioning.

IMPACTS OF TRAUMA

Classic PTSD symptoms exhibited by an individual experiencing trauma include the following:

- *Intrusive recollections*
  Replaying the trauma
  Flashbacks
  Ruminating about the event
  Nightmares
- *Numbing or withdrawal*
  Loss of interest in people and activities

Difficulty in feeling positive emotions
Avoidance of activities or places reminding one of the event
- *Hyperarousal*
Difficulty sleeping
Decreased concentration
Increased startle reaction
Always on edge

These symptoms are, however, only the tip of the iceberg. Particularly when children are chronically subjected to trauma, the impact expands from the symptoms noted above to a broad impact on the child's emotional development. For example, emotional trauma can impair a child's ability to learn to control and contain feelings in appropriate ways. The intense distress the child has experienced, the resulting anxiety and fear of the world, and the reservoir of pain that is left interfere with developing age-expected levels of self-control. Stressful events that most children could deal with and grow from overwhelm the traumatized child. Rather than mastery of the stressful situation, the child experiences retraumatization. Current stresses are magnified because they are fed by the reservoirs of painful memories, and because the child never learned to deal with this type of stressful event.

Traumatic events can profoundly impact a child's self-image and identity. Following such events, some children see the world as far more dangerous than they did previously. They then feel weak and vulnerable. Alternatively, a child may identify with the aggressor.

Social emotional skills are impaired, both because of the flood of anxiety and anger that arises and because the traumatized child's ability to learn can often be crippled. Cathy not only needed assistance in resolving her traumatic memories but needed a great deal of help in learning social and academic skills, in which she had lagged behind her peers, and help with her self-esteem and core identity. She needed a great deal of assistance to re-create an image in her mind of herself as able to succeed and deserving of success.

Children who experience trauma have a greater likelihood of experiencing future trauma. Once traumatized, people often suffer so much anxiety during future threatening situations that they are not able to think as carefully as they would have previously. Therefore, their ability to deal with threatening situations is compromised. The impacts of trauma may be summarized as follows:

- *Impaired emotional development*
  Weakened control over emotions
  Impulsiveness
  Irritability
  Rage
- *Problems of identity development*
  Revenge fantasies
  Identification with the aggressor
  Guilt
  Sense of vulnerability
  Foreshortened image of the future
- *Impaired social skills: changed images of the world*
  World is impossibly dangerous
  Hurt or be hurt
- *Increased vulnerability to future trauma*
  Learned helplessness—decreased ability to avoid dangerous situations
  Sensitization—decreased threshold for being frightened and overwhelmed by situations

WHAT SCHOOLS CAN DO

Social emotional educational efforts promote the psychosocial capacity that fosters children's resiliency. As such, they represent a primary prevention intervention. Purposefully promoting children's social and emotional literacy before a trauma occurs enhances their capacity to recognize what they are experiencing and to reflect on self and interpersonal experience. Systemic interventions that create safer, more caring and responsive homes and schools are, by definition, the optimal culture to prepare children (and adults) to deal with trauma.

When a child has been traumatized, social emotional educational efforts reduce the risk that the trauma will become a more severe and a psychically undermining experience. It is more likely that others will notice and reach out to children who have been wounded. Traumatized children often feel and act like victims and are more vulnerable to being bullied. Social emotional educational efforts always include antibullying efforts and focus on the bully-victim-bystander dynamic.

Social emotional educational efforts support adults' capacity to understand their own needs, which supports their ability to be attuned to children. These efforts necessarily pay attention to safety—social and emotional as well as physical.

WHAT INDIVIDUAL EDUCATORS CAN DO

Recognize Trauma

Recognizing trauma is often very difficult, since the symptoms mimic those of other psychological problems, and children are generally very reluctant to talk about either being traumatized or how it has affected them. Studies show that pediatricians recognize only one in four cases of childhood trauma and school guidance counselors only one in two. Failing to recognize who has been hurt and getting them help can, however, have very serious consequences for their lives.

Children who have suffered trauma are often misdiagnosed. They may appear simply to be depressed, or to have an anxiety disorder or be more aggressive than they had been. Moreover, the poor concentration and being on edge lead many to think of ADHD rather than trauma. Oppositional defiant disorder and conduct disorder can also be fostered by trauma. Following trauma, the anger and anxiety people feel can lead them to be oppositional, to object to anyone telling them what to do. Even bipolar disorder and psychosis can be mimicked by PTSD.

The most important sign of trauma is a significant change in behavior. One child will become much quieter and more withdrawn than usual. Another child will become aggressive, agitated, hyperactive, and reckless. The next will become anxious and clingy. Another will become distracted and seem a million miles away. Many will have headaches or stomachaches. The crucial issue is not whether the child is quieter than most children or more active than most children. The issue is the change in the child's behavior from the baseline. We should not assume that a child becoming moody or quiet is simply going through a phase. The primary things that Cathy's parents and teachers saw was that she became quiet and her school performance slid.

A key sign that some children will show is joyless, driven, repetitive play. This may involve drawing the painful memory over and over again, acting it out with dolls, or playing it out with other children. Children who have been sexually abused or prematurely exposed to sexual material will often engage in sexual play or bullying. The child may become preoccupied with sexual issues, inappropriately touch other children, make inappropriate sexualized comments, or behave in inappropriate sexual ways.

Respond Effectively to Trauma

To ascertain whether trauma has occurred and to effectively respond to a child's traumatic experience, an educator or caregiver needs to do the following:

1. Be attentive and observant to children's schoolwork, play, and behavior, as these activities may be potential signs of their problems.
2. Respectfully, gently, and supportively show interest in a child's feelings to build trust so the child can easily talk with the adult.

3. Acknowledge the child's feelings and physical responses (i.e., crying) to help the child become aware of what he or she is feeling.
4. Avoid being dismissive or condescending toward the child's feelings and reactions to the traumatic experience.
5. Use open-ended and nonjudgmental questions and comments to talk with child about how certain feelings are leading to problematic behavior.
6. Work together to find more appropriate ways to deal with feelings.
7. Avoid probing for traumatic experiences or details of an instance that the child reveals. That task is for a mental health professional.
8. Identify an appropriate individual or agency to assist the child and his or her family with assessment and any needed follow-up counseling.

When in doubt, seek expert guidance.

Refer a Child

Sometimes we are not sure when to contact a school- or community-based mental health professional. As noted above, if we are wondering whether we should refer a child for treatment, it is probably wise to confer with a knowledgeable colleague or a mental health professional. In fact, educators have a legal obligation to report suspected abuse to proper authorities.

The vignette about Cathy at the beginning of this chapter is a disturbing common instance that powerfully underscores the importance of educators contacting a qualified mental health professional when a child or teenager may be in trouble. The only signs of trauma others could readily see were Cathy's withdrawal and declining grades. She seemed to not care about things she used to find important and had a harder time enjoying things than she had previously. She did not tell anyone she was thinking about suicide, but it was on her mind. Many children and adolescents

nonverbally signal that they are in trouble—they begin to withdraw. We sense that something has shifted, but we do not know
what and the student does not tell us. There are three signals that
are always important to pay attention and respond to: suicidal
statements or jokes; relatively rapid changes in student functioning; and failure to gradually improve when a student has been
traumatized and people recognize this. When we provide adequate support, students do gradually begin to improve (e.g., relationally, moodwise, and/or academically). When this does not occur, it may signal that something is complicating the process of
mourning and healing.

It is always important to take any and all student statements
about suicide seriously. Sometimes, jokes about suicide are simply
jokes. But sometimes they are not. Whether the educator asks the
student directly or goes to an administrator or school-based mental health professional, these kinds of statements need to be addressed. We need to ask students directly how they are feeling
and what is feeling okay and not so okay. Again, as educators, we
need to pay attention to our feelings during this kind of conversation. Sometimes, we will feel very clearly that the student's response indicates that this was just a joke. On the other hand,
sometimes we may be left with a queasy, anxious feeling that this
is serious. In these instances, it is essential that we confer with a
knowledgeable colleague and mental health professional.

In other instances, there are no dire statements, joking or not,
but we see a change in student behavior. If a student's social life
or academic work takes a sudden turn, we need to notice this and
again, directly or indirectly talk to the student in an open, caring
and curious way: "What's going on?" Again, we need to pay attention to how we feeland to the extent that we feel anxious, it is
essential to talk with a knowledgeable colleague or mental health
professional.

Finally, we may know that a student who was traumatized is
not resolving the traumatic experience, and it is continuing to interfere with some aspect of life. This can be complicated. For example, students who have been traumatized commonly go through
psychotherapy as an important part of the healing process. Some-

times, even when we believe that the match between clinician and student is a good one and that progress is being made, students understandably continue to show signs that they are hurting. Naturally, these residual feelings can complicate learning and social life. What is most important is not to assume that if a student is in psychotherapy that the problem is fixed. To the extent that we are connected with such a student, we need to periodically check in and let the student know we care and we are paying attention. When we see students stuck with the same difficulties months after the trauma, whether they are in psychotherapy or not, we need to intervene and do our best to discover how they feel and what they need.

SUMMARY

In this chapter, we have made the following points:

- A significant percentage of children suffer emotional trauma.
- Without assistance, traumatized children will have marked impairment in their ability to learn and will often disrupt others' attempts to learn.
- Trauma can lead to agitation and aggressiveness or to anxiety and clinginess, to withdrawal and numbing, or to inappropriate sexual behavior.
- Even skilled clinicians often fail to realize that underneath a child's anxiety, depression, oppositional behavior, aggression, hyperactivity, or difficulty concentrating is a history of trauma or high levels of current stress.
- A significant change in behavior is the key sign of trauma.
- Chronic trauma, in particular, has a profound impact on emotional development, including identity, images of the world, and a person's ability to learn to contain and correctly express emotions.
- Effective treatments for trauma have been developed in recent years. Traumatized children should be referred to people specially trained to deal with trauma.

- By recognizing the signs of trauma and referring children, schools can do an enormous service to traumatized children and improve the learning environment.

REFLECTING ON YOUR CURRENT PRACTICE

There are many possible signs of trauma. As you reflect on students you know who have been traumatized, or that you suspect are traumatized, consider the following signs of possible trauma:

- Does the student show disruption in peer relationships, as indicated by conflict or isolation?
- Has there been a significant decrease in school performance and concentration?
- Do you hear about ongoing physical complaints with no apparent cause?
- Have you seen an increased use of chemical substances and alcohol?
- Has the student reported or talked about repeated nightmares or other problems sleeping, strong fears of death, violence, and so on?
- Have you seen indications of a drop in self-esteem?
- Have you seen a general lack of energy and interest in previously enjoyed activities?
- Have you seen tantrums and other persistent controlling and aggressive behaviors, irritability, and uncontrollable rage attacks?
- Does the student present with blunted emotions?
- Has the student become hyperactive or shown an exaggerated startle reflex?
- Has the student become forgetful?
- Is the student showing excessive belligerence or shyness, withdrawal or fearfulness?
- In the case of a young child, has he or she been playing repetitively, reenacting traumatic events?
- Has the young child become very anxious about separation or clingy?

CHAPTER EIGHT

Promoting Learning and Safety in School: A Model and Process

Southeastern High will reopen with only freshmen in the fall semester of next year. Today was the last day of the school year, and it was the last day students would be able to attend this failing school. Nevertheless, the students could not tear themselves away. They sat in the cafeteria and signed one another's notebooks and talked about the future with their teachers and the assistant principals.

The City Board of Education voted in January to close down the historic building and to reopen next year with five new small schools with freshmen only. At each school, a grade will be added each year to make five smaller schools. The school ranks lowest in the city's academic assessment program and has an abysmal graduation rate. More than 90% of its students qualify for free or reduced-price lunch. The streets surrounding the school are filled with litter and lined with abandoned buildings. The 4,500 students who have attended Southeastern High will be displaced by this decision and will have to go to other schools of their choice around the city. Administrators say that the students will mostly go to Southern High, which has many of the same problems as their current school. Many of their teachers will follow them to the same school. Others will find jobs with the Board of Education. As a principal of one of the five new schools, your challenge is to bring all of the stakeholders together—teachers, students, parents, counselors, and other school staff—to establish the academic, social, emotional, and ethical climate for this new institution.

To a greater or lesser extent, all school leaders and leadership teams are invested in school improvement. In this final chapter, we suggest a model for improving school climate that integrates research from risk prevention, K–12 education, physical and mental health promotion, social emotional learning, and character education.

Although educators have appreciated the importance of school climate for almost 100 years (Perry, 1908), there is no universally accepted definition. The terms *School climate* and *school culture* often overlap. Practitioners and researchers use a range of terms such as *atmosphere, feelings, tone, setting,* or *milieu* (Freiberg, 1999; Tagiuri, 1968). In essence, school climate refers to our subjective experience in school. As such, school climate recognizes and reflects people's social, emotional, ethical, and cognitive experience (Cohen, 2006). Positive school climate refers to a safe, caring, responsive, and participatory place for students and teachers to learn, teach, and develop in healthy ways.

The process of improving the social, emotional, ethical, and academic school climate brings the community together to understand the current strengths and challenges to school safety in order to promote learning and the healthy development of K–12 students. Our model for improving your school's climate involves a practical strategy that recognizes and integrates the issues we have outlined in the previous chapters. The model has five stages: planning, data gathering and evaluation, interpreting the data and action planning, implementation, and reevaluation and further planning. We detail (1) what each stage is, (2) why it is important, (3) the tasks that need to be addressed in each stage, (4) the indicators of success, and (5) a series of questions for reflection.

STAGE 1. PLANNING: CREATING THE FOUNDATION

What Is It?

- Bringing key stakeholders together: inspiring leadership and evaluation teams

- Reflecting on past efforts and current needs, including crisis management
- Reflecting on short- and long-term goals
- Creating evaluation plans to support an authentic learning community

Why Is This Stage Important?

- Creating leadership teams that represent the community provides the foundation for effective school reform.
- The crisis team and school safety committee can be re-energized.
- Top-down leadership by itself fails. What is needed is bottom-up and top-down working together.

Tasks at This Stage

- Form a diverse leadership team representing key stakeholder groups including teachers and parents, as well as key leaders in the community from business, faith-based agencies, youth development organizations, and governmental agencies.
- Develop inclusive guidelines and procedures for working together as a team.
- Revisit the school mission. Discuss the specific ways in which the mission statement is and is not a reality in the school. Explicitly talk about how your school, like all schools, has strengths, weaknesses, needs, and emerging goals that grow out of its history and current reality.
- Understand the five-stage social, emotional, ethical, and academic school improvement process outlined above.
- Discuss how the school improvement initiatives might address gaps between the school's mission and reality.
- State preliminary goals for the school improvement initiative.
- Anticipate potential challenges that may prevent staff, students, parents, and community members from coming together to support school improvement efforts:

Time constraints: Finding the time to plan and discuss the process of substantive and sustained school
improvement is difficult.
Fear: School leaders know that unhappy members of
the school community may want to use evaluation
findings to prove their point.
Creation of teams that really represent the school
community, particularly traditionally marginalized
groups.
- Develop a preliminary strategy to address these challenges, including a plan for introducing and getting input from students, parents, and teachers on the initiatives outlined.

Indicators of Success at This Stage

- The school has an inclusive, representative leadership
team.
- The school has a plan for introducing and gathering input from all constituents regarding the school improvement initiatives.
- Students, staff, and parents feel that their needs and interests are being heard.
- School staff understand that all schools have strengths
and weaknesses; what is important is to recognize the
need to develop collaborative plans for school improvement.
- School staff appreciate that change is difficult and
takes place over time.
- School staff have clear goals for the initiatives.

Questions for Reflection

1. Does planning really make a difference?
2. What are my doubts and hopes for this stage?
3. What do I have to contribute to the success of this
stage?

4. What do others have to contribute? How will I tap into these potential contributions?
5. What's in it for students, teachers, parents, staff, administrators, and the wider school community?
6. What will really make this stage a success?
7. What are the major challenges to an effective and collaborative planning process?
8. What are the most important tips or strategies that I wish I had known about before embarking on this kind of planning process?

STAGE 2. DATA GATHERING AND EVALUATION

What Is It?

- Evaluating the school's strengths and weaknesses pedagogically and systemically with a scientifically sound school climate measure that assesses how all members of the community feel about school life. Educational research has revealed that there are ten overlapping dimensions that color and shape our experience in schools or school climate (Cohen, 2006):
    1. Environmental (cleanliness; adequate space and materials; inviting aesthetic quality)
    2. Structural (size of school; curricular and extracurricular offerings)
    3. Safety—physical (crisis plan, clearly communicated rules, clear and consistent violation response, people in the school feel physically safe, attitudes about violence); and social emotional (attitudes about individual differences, students' and adults' attitudes about and responses to bullying, conflict resolution taught in school, belief in school rules)
    4. Teaching and learning (high expectations for student achievement; all learning styles honored; help provided when needed; learning linked to daily life; engaging materials; use of praise and reward;

opportunities for participation; varied teaching
methods; instructional leadership; creativity valued; social emotional as well as academic learning
valued and taught; varied types of intelligence appreciated; connections across disciplines)
5. Relationships (positive adult-adult relationships between teachers, administrators, and staff; positive
adult-student relationships; positive student-student
relationships; shared decision making; common academic planning opportunities; diversity valued; student participation in learning and discipline)
6. Sense of school community (students and adults feel
and demonstrate a sense of community in the school)
7. Morale (students are engaged learners; staff are en-
thusiastic about their work; students are connected
to one or more adults; students and staff feel good
about school)
8. Peer norms (students and staff feel learning is important; are invested in caring; appreciate importance of being able to say no; expect collaboration
and cooperation)
9. School-home-community partnerships (mutual support and ongoing communication; school-commu-
nity involvement; parent participation in school
decision making; shared parent-teacher norms vis-
à-vis learning and behavior; student family assistance programs)
10. Learning community (standards and measures
used to support learning and continuous improvement; professional development systematic and ongoing; data-driven decision making linked to learning; school systems evaluated)
• Selecting an appropriate school climate survey (see Cohen, 2006, for a summary). Only two K–12 school climate tools are scientifically sound and comprehensive
in two ways: assessing students, parents, and school
personnel as well as evaluating all of the dimensions
that scholars and practitioners believe define school

climate. We recommend (1) HiPlaces Measure (Felner et al., 2001) and (2) the Comprehensive School Climate Inventory (for details, see www.csee.net/climate/csciassessment/; Sandy, Cohen, & Fisher, 2006). There are also school climate tools developed in scientifically sound ways that focus on character education–related issues (CHARACTER Plus, 2002) or diversity (Holt & Keyes, 2003).

Why Is This Stage Important?

- Scientifically sound and multiple evaluation measures provide a realistic snapshot of current strengths and challenges.
- Uses a 360-degree measure (i.e., a tool assessing how students, parents, and school personnel experience school life) that gathers perceptions of all stakeholders, including parents, students, teachers, staff, and administrators.
- When parents and students are involved with this initial assessment, their voices are being heard.
- Examining your school's strengths and weaknesses both pedagogically and systemically helps you learn what is and is not working and serves as a springboard for change.
- Establishing baseline data is an important way of assessing growth.

Tasks at This Stage

- The leadership team works in collaboration with all stakeholder groups to create an effective, inclusive plan for administering the school climate tool.
- The leadership team facilitates administration of the school climate tool in a timely way and gathers additional baseline data (e.g., attendance data, dropout rates,

academic information, and teacher and administrator turnover rate).

- The leadership team ensures that a representative number of parents complete the school climate measure. It is relatively easy to ensure that students and school personnel will complete this measure, as they are a captive audience in school. It is much more challenging, but essential, that a large group of parents complete these assessment tools too.
- The leadership team anticipates possible challenges that may inadvertently thwart staff, students, parents, and community members from coming together to participate in data gathering. Some parents may find completing the survey intimidating or time consuming, or feel that it is unlikely to result in significant change. Some in the school community may have been discouraged by the failure of other school initiatives. Some groups may believe that it is not their place to voice their views and will trust the school to do what is best.
- The leadership team collaboratively develops and implements strategies to address these challenges.
- The school receives a narrative, numerical, and graphic report based on the surveys.
- The leadership team promotes an understanding that evaluation is always a step in a longer-term process of school improvement. Assessment does not provide simple answers.

Indicators of Success at This Stage

- A representative majority of parents, students, teachers, staff, and administrators have completed the school climate and other measures.
- The school leadership team has received the school climate report that describes and summarizes the school's strengths and challenges from student, staff, and parental perspectives.
- There is consensus in the school community that

enough information was provided about the school climate measure, as well as satisfactory time and opportunities to complete it.

- The leadership team informs the school community when the results of the survey will be shared with them.

Questions for Reflection

1. What skills and dispositions do I have that I can draw on as a leader that will help me inspire and mobilize the school community to complete the evaluation measures?
2. How can members of the school community consistently honor what we have accomplished, and how can we appreciate those who have helped contribute to the success of this stage?
3. How will I respond to the report? Am I open? Defensive?
4. With so much on my plate, am I really committed to seeing this stage as one step in a long-term school improvement process? What do we hope to gain in the long term?
5. How do we keep the momentum for this initiative going, given everything else that we have to do?
6. What are the most important challenges for this stage of the school improvement model?
7. What have I found to be the most helpful and concrete strategies to ensure that parents are a part of this process?

STAGE 3. INTERPRETATION OF THE DATA AND ACTION PLANNING

What Is It?

- Understanding the initial assessment findings.
- Using these findings to develop an evidence-based ac-

tion plan to promote social, emotional, ethical, and academic learning as well as a secure climate for learning.

Why Is This Stage Important?

- Assessment findings are useful only if they are understood and used.
- Too often evaluation findings are not understood and are quickly shelved.
- Providing time for staff, students, and parents to respectfully think about and communicate their thoughts and feelings about the findings is essential for building community and taking the next step. This is challenging for many reasons. For one thing, there never seems to be enough time. But even more important, various members of the community have very different points of view. Parents, for example, are often relatively difficult to engage, for many reasons. Cultural differences can exist between a group of parents on the one hand and educators on the other. In a growing number of American communities, some parents are afraid of coming to the school because they are not documented citizens. Some parents feel too busy to bother. In any case, to the extent that school leaders do not effectively reach out to all members of the community, it will undermine this process of school improvement.
- Setting priorities together can promote student and parent participation and can create a shared vision and a common vocabulary. This is the optimal foundation for sustained school improvement.
- Promoting student participation as well as parent-school partnerships enhances students' inclination to learn and develop in healthy ways.
- The school climate report may evoke a range of emotions. In a safe context, expressing and witnessing emotional storytelling helps members of the school community to connect with one another in deep and powerful ways that may motivate them to make needed changes.

Tasks at This Stage

There are four major tasks at this stage: (1) understanding and digging deeper into the school climate report and related data, (2) setting priorities, (3) developing an action plan, and (4) anticipating challenges.

Understanding and digging deeper into the comprehensive school climate report.

- The school leader, with the school leadership team, reviews the school climate report and develops a short-term plan to engage each stakeholder group—parents, students, teachers, administrators, and staff—to dig deeper into the findings.
- School leaders remind the community that all schools have strengths and weaknesses and assessment is just one step in the school improvement process.
- School leaders meet with staff, students, and parents to talk about these findings. These meetings present an opportunity for community building and the promotion of student and parent participation. Possible focus questions for these sessions:
  1. What in the report resonates for you? What feelings emerge for you?
  2. What do you find surprising about this report?
  3. Do you have a story to share that might help us learn more about your personal experiences related to an issue raised in this report?
  4. What issues that emerge from this report seem most important to address?

Setting priorities. As an outgrowth of understanding the evaluation findings, the school leadership needs to identify one systemic and one pedagogical goal to focus on for the first 2 years. We suggest using the most inclusive and democratic process possible. Goals need to be aligned with the school's mission and coordinated with the school's other initiatives.

Developing an action plan.

- The leadership team needs to synthesize the priorities that have emerged from staff, student, and parent discussions.
- Subgroups conduct research about evidence-based best practices that the school might implement to address these priority areas.
- Each stakeholder group develops implementation options from which they can choose and that fit well with their roles and other responsibilities.
- The leadership team works with each stakeholder group to list the resources and assets the school community now has to address the priority goals.
- This action plan is conceptualized as a 3- to 5-year problem-solving cycle. Here the school is defining an initial set of goals that will be periodically reevaluated, learned from, and built on.
- The action plan includes a clear evaluation plan.

Anticipating possible challenges.

- Time constraints: Schools are busy places. Finding the time to meet and discuss initial findings is a significant challenge.
- Cynicism and burnout: Some members of the school community may feel and say, in essence, "We have tried this. It won't work."
- Collaborative planning is difficult work. Collaboration is more or less difficult depending on (1) the collaborative task, (2) the social emotional skills and dispositions of the collaborators, and (3) the meanings that people attribute to the collaborative process.
- Working and learning with members of the school community is inherently a difficult collaborative endeavor. It takes a deep commitment to school improvement and social, emotional, ethical, and academic educational goals to sustain this work. Dictatorship is always an easier leadership style in the short run.

- Fear and courage: It is inherently scary for school leaders to embark on a truly collaborative, democratic process of school improvement. We cannot and do not know what will happen. It takes great courage to be a social, emotional, ethical, and academic school leader.
- Taking on too much: We often get excited about wonderful ideas but must try to develop a realistic action plan that can be implemented without being discouraging.

Indicators of Success at This Stage

- A plan for understanding and digging deeper, sharing stories, and setting priorities based on the school climate findings has been successfully implemented.
- There is general consensus, based on anecdotal and formal feedback, that this stage has been well organized, respectful, and has helped to build community.
- Teams have been given time to research best practices and current school assets related to the two priority goals established during this stage.
- A preliminary written action plan has been developed and shared with the school community for feedback.
- A final action plan has been completed and communicated to the school community.
- The action plan is aligned with evidence-based guidelines.
- Members of the school community have been individually and publicly thanked for their participation in this stage.

Questions for Reflection

- What, if anything, was most meaningful and moving about the process of understanding and digging deeper?
- In what ways was this process different and more successful than other forums we have had?
- How were traditionally marginalized voices (e.g., members of minority groups) brought forward?

- What did not work well in this stage and what lessons did we learn?
- What did I learn about myself during this process?
- Which of my assumptions about the school and its different stakeholders shifted? In what ways?
- Have we taken on too much?
- What action plan models or templates have I found to be most helpful?

STAGE 4. IMPLEMENTATION OF THE ACTION PLAN

What Is It?

- Evidence-based pedagogical and systemic efforts designed to (1) promote students' social, emotional, and cognitive competencies and ethical dispositions; and (2) systemically create safe, caring, and responsive schools.
- A 3- to 5-year effort.

Why Is This Stage Important?

- When implementation is done over a 3- to 5-year period, we promote academic achievement, school success, and violence prevention through sustained effort, evaluation, reflection, and revision.
- Implementing evidence-based pedagogic and systemic efforts (1) promotes students' social, emotional, and cognitive competencies and ethical dispositions; and (2) creating a climate for learning.
- We promote the skills, knowledge, and dispositions that provide the foundation for life success: being able to love, work, and participate in a democratic society.

Tasks at This Stage

- The leadership team facilitates the implementation process, providing the needed time, space, and other resources for success.

- Members of different stakeholder groups work on aspects of the implementation plan.
- Implementation groups communicate with each other and offer "critical friends" support on a regular basis, for example, supportive pairings of teachers who observe one another teaching and think collaboratively about how to promote even more effective instructional methods (Dunne, Nave, & Lewis, 2000).
- The leadership team communicates and shows the progress of the implementation plan to the school community.
- The leadership team facilitates and monitors ongoing assessment of the action plan.
- A school improvement coordinator is designated. This coordinator will be given time and support to actually coordinate this effort.
- New staff, parents, and students receive an orientation to the school improvement initiative and are welcomed and engaged in the implementation process.
- Potential challenges are recognized, and a preliminary strategy is developed to address these challenges.
  1. Staff and administrative turnover may make it difficult to sustain the initiative.
  2. Implementation results may not show immediate results.
  3. Current sources of funds may dry up and new sources need to be found.
  4. The person designated as the coordinator does not actually have time or support to perform in this role.

Indicators of Success at This Stage

- Each staff member and the student body are engaged in implementing a self-selected aspect of the implementation plan.
- Groups of parents are implementing self-selected parts of the plan and have successfully kept the action plan timeline and fulfilled their responsibilities.

- Adequate resources are allocated to support implementation efforts.
- The coordinator is actually coordinating this effort and being an ongoing learner and teacher about the process.
- Members of the school community celebrate their own and each other's progress.

Questions for Reflection

1. How can we celebrate ongoing progress and at the same time make the necessary shifts when they are needed?
2. How can we keep our on focus on the students?
3. Can we resist adding further goals without removing some other task?
4. In what ways can we support each other when things get rough?
5. What are practical and informative methods to track the implementation process that supports authentic and continuous learning?

STAGE 5. REEVALUATION AND FURTHER PLANNING

What Is It?

- Reevaluating the school's strengths and challenges
- Discovering what has changed and what has helped to further the school improvement process
- Learning about what has not changed and the barriers to school improvement
- Revising plans to improve the school socially, emotionally, ethically, and academically

Why Is This Stage Important?

- Although schools may have an anecdotal and intuitive sense about how the initiative is progressing, it is important to gather multiple forms of assessment data on an ongoing basis and every 12 to 24 months.

- Data can help pinpoint areas that have made improvement and those that need further work or different strategies.

Tasks at This Stage

- At 9 to 24 months, the school climate measure and any number of other measures are readministered to obtain data showing gains in areas that have been the focus of the school improvement initiative.
- Other data, such as attendance, dropout rate, and academic achievement, are gathered and discussed with respect to the school climate data.
- The leadership team synthesizes the assessment information as it relates to the implementation effort and shares it with each of the constituent groups.
- Action plans are revised slightly in response to the evaluation data.

Indicators of Success at This Stage

- The school climate measure as well as other possible tools have been readministered and stakeholder groups have discussed the report. Success is celebrated and plans are made to address challenges.
- The school community can feel positive subtle and more obvious changes in the school's climate in areas that have been the focus of the action plan.

Questions for Reflection

1. Who in particular has contributed to the success of this initiative? What are the attributes of their contribution? What can we learn?
2. Do we take time to celebrate what is working?
3. Who owns this initiative?
4. How might we continue to expand the ownership of this effort?

SUMMARY

In this final chapter, we have outlined a process of school climate improvement that builds on research and best practices from K–12 education, social emotional learning, character education, risk prevention, and physical and mental health. It is a process anchored in two essential goals that prevent physical, social, and emotional violence as well as promoting health: (1) purposefully promoting social, emotional, and cognitive competencies as well as ethical dispositions over time; and (2) creating a climate for learning or a positive school climate.

The five-stage school climate cycle that we have outlined here is a road map of sorts. It is a series of tasks and frameworks that support community-wide learning and change. In doing so, we are truly making schools safer physically, socially, and emotionally. We are creating a true community of learners and teachers who are invested in listening to themselves and others. There is a wide range of school climate improvement issues that we have not explored here. For example, we have not described assessing readiness for change, identifying curricula that may address your school's goals and needs, school climate policy, the range of costs and state as well as federal funding sources, and the range of barriers to school climate improvement, as well as lessons learned from practitioners and research. The Center for Social and Emotional Education is committed to supporting a larger community of learners and teachers to further understanding, evaluating, and positively shaping school climate. Our Web site (www.csee.net) has information about all of these issues and more. Perhaps most important, it provides a forum where we can learn from one another about how to foster substantive and sustained school climate improvement.

The process of school climate improvement promotes the skills and dispositions that provide the foundation for participation in a democracy (Cohen, 2006; Cohen & Michelli, 2006). It is interesting to think about what it means to be a member of a democracy. There is a series of skills: learning to listen to ourselves and others; being able to think in critical and reflective ways; being able to solve problems and conflicts and make decisions flexibly, creatively, and nonviolently; and being able to communicate and collaborate with others. Being an engaged member of a democracy also entails a series of dispositions: being responsible; appreciating that we are social creatures and need others to survive and thrive; appreciating that a nation is only as strong as its weakest members; and appreciating that it is an honor and a pleasure to serve and help others.

Making your school safe—socially, emotionally, and physically—has to involve more than a violence prevention curriculum or intervention. To be safe, we need to know that others care and will notice. To do so necessarily involves promoting a caring and democratic community. It is extraordinary that we now have research-based guidelines to do just this (American Psychological Association, 2003; Berkowitz & Bier, 2005; Greenberg et al., 2003). Yet, so often we do not translate these research findings into practice. Our children deserve better. The country deserves better.

References

Allen, J. P., Weissberg, R. P., & Hawkins, J. A. (1989). The relation between values and social competence in early adolescence. *Developmental Psychology, 25*(3), 458–464.

American Psychological Association. (2003). Presidential task force on prevention, promoting strength, resilience, and health in young people. *American Psychologist, 58,* 425–490.

Ballard, M., Tucky, A., & Remley, Jr., T. P. (1999, May). Bullying and school violence: A proposed intervention program. NASSP Bulletin, 83(6–7), 38–47.

Bar-On, R. (2005). The impact of emotional-social intelligence on subjective well-being. *Perspectives in Education, 23*(2), 41–61.

Bar-On, R., Maree, J. G., & Elias, M. J. (2006). *Educating people to be emotionally intelligent.* Johannesburg, South Africa: Heinemann Publishers.

Berkowitz, M. W., & Bier, M. C. (2005). *What works in character education: A report for policy makers and opinion leaders.* Character Education Partnership. Retrieved September 10, 2005, from http://www.character. org/atf/cf/{77B36AC3-5057-4795-8A8F-9B2FCB86F3EB}/practitioners_518.pdf.

Black, S. (2004). Beyond zero tolerance: Schools don't need extreme policies to be safe and secure. *American School Board Journal, 191*(9), 62–64.

Blum, R. W., McNeely, C. A., & Rinehart, P. M. (2002). *Improving the odds: The untapped power of schools to improve the health of teens.* Minneapolis: University of Minnesota, Center for Adolescent Health and Development.

Bowman, D. H. (2001). At school, a cruel culture. *Education Week, 20*(27), 1, 16.

Caprara, V., Barbanelli, C., Pastorelli, C., Bandura, A., & Zimbardo, P. (2000, July). Prosocial foundations of children's academic achievement. *Psychological Science, 11*(4), 302–306.

Caroline, T. H. (1905). *The ethical culture school—its past.* Unpublished manuscript, Tate Library, Fieldston School, Riverdale, NY.

Catalano, R. F., Berglund, M. L., Ryan, J. A. M., Lonczak, H. S., & Hawkins, D. (2002). Positive youth development in the United States: Research findings on evaluations of positive youth development programs [Electronic version]. *Prevention and Treatment, 5*(1). Retrieved January 12, 2003, from http://journals.apa.org/prevention/volume5/pre0050015a.html.

Catalano, R. F., Haggerty, K. P., Oesterie, S., Fleming, C. B., & Hawkins, J. D. (2004). The importance of bonding to schools for healthy development: Findings from the social development research group. *Journal of School Health, 74*(7), 252–262.

Chapell, M. S., Hasselman, S., Kitchin, T., Lomon, S. N., & Sarullo, P. L. (2006).

Bullying in elementary school, high school and college. *Adolescence, 41*, pp. 633–648.

CHARACTER Plus. (2002). *Character evaluation resource guide: Tools and strategies for evaluating a character education program.* St. Louis, MO: Author.

Cohen, J. (Ed.). (1999). *Educating minds and hearts: Social emotional learning and the passage into adolescence.* New York: Teachers College Press.

Cohen, J. (2001). Social and emotional education: Core concepts and practices. In J. Cohen (Ed.), *Caring classrooms/intelligent schools: The social emotional education of young children* (pp. 3–29). New York: Teachers College Press.

Cohen, J. (2006). Social, emotional, ethical, and academic education: Creating a climate for learning, participation in democracy, and well-being. *Harvard Educational Review, 76*(2), 201–237.

Cohen, J., & Sandy, S. (2003). Perspectives in social-emotional education: Theoretical foundations and new evidence-based developments in current practice. *Perspectives in Education, 21*(4), 41–54.

Cohen, J., & Michelli, N. M. (2006). Evaluating school climate: Promoting the skills, dispositions and a climate for democracy. *NNER (National Network for Educational Renewal) News, 6*(1), 2–4.

Collaborative for Academic, Social and Emotional Learning. (2003, March). *Safe and sound: An educational leader's guide to evidence-based social and emotional (SEL) programs.* Chicago: Collaborative for Academic, Social, and Emotional Learning.

Commonwealth Fund Survey of the Health of Adolescent Girls. (1997). Available at http://www.cmwf.org/publications/publications_show.htm?doc_id= 221230.

Dunne, F., Nave, B., & Lewis, A. (2000). Critical Friends Groups: Teachers helping teachers to improve student learning. *Phi Delta Kappa*, Research Bulletin, *28*, p. 4.

Edleson, J. L. (1999). Children's witnessing of adult domestic violence. *Journal of Interpersonal Violence, 14*(8), 839–870.

Elias, M. J., & Arnold, H. (2006). *The educator's guide to emotional intelligence and academic achievement: Social-emotional learning in the classroom.* Thousand Oaks, CA: Corwin Press.

Elliott, D., Beatrix H., & Kirk, R. W. (1998). *Violence in American schools: A new perspective.* New York: Cambridge University Press.

ERIC. (2001). *Zero-tolerance policies.* ERIC Digest 146, Clearinghouse on Educational Management, U.S. Department of Education. Available at http://eric.uoregon.edu/publications/digests/digest146.html

Farberman, R. (2006). Zero tolerance policies can have unintended effects, APP report finds. *Monitor in Psychology, 37*(9), 27.

Farrington, D. P. Understanding and preventing bullying. *Crime and Justice, 17*, 381–458.

Felner, R. D., Favazza, A., Shim, M., Brand, S., Gu, K., & Shim, N. (2001). Whole school improvement and restructuring as prevention and promotion: Lessons from STEP and the Project on High Performance Learning Communities. *Journal of School Psychology, 39*(2), 177–202.

Fitzpatrick, K. M., & Boldizar, J. (1993). The prevalence and consequences of exposure to violence among African-American youth. *Journal of the American Academy of Child & Adolescent Psychiatry, 32*(2), 424–430.

Fredericks, L. (2003). *Making the case for social and emotional learning and service learning.* Denver: Education Commission of the States. Available at www.ecs.org.

Freiberg, H. J. (Ed.). (1999). *School climate: Measuring, improving and sustaining healthy learning environments.* Philadelphia: Falmer.

Fuchs-Nadeau, D., LaRue, C. M., Allen, J., Cohen, J., & Hyman, L. (2002). *The New York State interpersonal violence prevention resource guide: Stopping youth violence before it begins.* Albany, NY: New York State Center for School Safety.

Goleman, D. (1995). *Emotional intelligence.* New York: Bantam Books.

Goleman, D. (1998). *Working with emotional intelligence.* New York: Bantam Books.

Greenberg, M. T., Weissberg, R. P., O'Brien, M. U., Zins, J. E., Fredericks, L., Resnik, H., et al. (2003). Enhancing school-based prevention and youth development through coordinated social, emotional, and academic learning. *American Psychologist, 58*(6/7), 466–474.

Guerra, N. G. (2003). Preventing school violence by promoting wellness. *Journal of Applied Psychoanalytic Studies, 5*(2), 139–154.

Hazler, R. J., Miller, D., Carney, J., & Green, S. (2001). Adult recognition of school bullying situations. *Educational Research, 43*, 133–146.

Heath, D. H. (1991). *Fulfilling lives: Paths to maturity and success.* San Francisco, CA: Jossey-Bass.

Holt, M. K., & Keyes, M. A. (2003). Teachers' attitudes toward bullying. In D. L. Espelage & S. M. Swearer (Eds.), *Bullying in American schools: A social-ecological perspective on prevention and intervention* (pp. 121–140). Hillsdale, NJ: Erlbaum.

Hoover, J., & Oliver, R. (1996). *The Bullying Prevention Handbook : A guide for principals, teachers, and counselors.* Bloomington, IN: National Education Service.

Hoven, C. W., Duarte, C. S., Lucas, C. P., Wu, P., Mandell, D. J., Goodwin, R. D., Cohen, M., Balaban, V., Woodruff, B. A., Fan, B., Mei, L., Musa, G. J., Cantor, P. A., Aber, J. L., Cohen, P., & Susser, E. (2005). Psychopathology among New York City school children six months after September 11th. *Archives of General Psychiatry, 62*(5), 545–551.

Huesmann, L. M., Guerra, N. G., Miller, L., & Zelli, A. (1992). The role of social norms in the development of aggression. In H. Zumkley & A. Fraczek (Eds.), *Socialization and aggression* (pp. 139–152). New York: Springer.

Hugh-Jones, S., & Smith, P. K. (1999). Self-reports of short- and long-term effects of bullying on children who stammer. *British Journal of Educational Psychology, 69*(2), 141–158.

Johnson, D. W., & Johnson, R. (1989). *Cooperation and competition: Theory and research.* Edina, MN: Interaction.

Karcher, M. J. (2002a). Connectedness and school violence: A framework for developmental interventions. In E. Gerler (Ed.), *Handbook of school violence* (pp. 7–40). Binghamton, NY: Haworth.

Karcher, M. J. (2002b). The cycle of violence and disconnection among rural middle school students: Teacher disconnectedness as a consequence of violence. *Journal of School Violence, 1*(1), 35–51.

Kaye, C. B. (2004). *The complete guide to service learning.* Minneapolis, MN: Free Spirit.

Kirby, D. (2001). Understanding what works and what doesn't in reducing adolescent risk taking. *Family Planning Perspectives, 33*(6), 276–281.

Lumsden, L. (2002). Preventing bullying. Eugene, OR: ERIC Clearinghouse on Educational Management ED-99-CO-0011.

Malik, N. M., Crowson, M. M., & Lederman, C. S. (2002). Evaluating maltreated infants, toddlers and preschoolers in dependency court. *Infant Mental Health Journal, 23*(5), 576–592.

Matthews, G., Zeidner, M., & Roberts, R. D. (2002). *Emotional intelligence: Science and myth.* Cambridge: MIT Press.

Mayer, J. D., & Salovey, P. (1997). What is emotional intelligence? In P. Salovey & D. J. Sluyter (Eds.), *Emotional development and emotional intelligence: Educational implications* (pp. 3–31). New York: Basic Books.

Nakasato, J. (2000). Data-based decision making in Hawaii's behavior support effort. *Journal of Positive Behavior Interventions, 2*, 247–251.

National Center on Child Abuse and Neglect. (1997). A PTSD Fact Sheet. American Humane Association. Available at www.ridalaskaofchildabuse.org/AHA_neg_abuse.html.

Parker, J. G., Rubin, K. H., Price, J. M., & DeRosier, M. E. (1995). Peer relationships, child development, and adjustment: A developmental psychopathology perspective. In D. Cicchetti & D. J. Cohen (Eds.), *Developmental psychopathology* (Vol. 2, pp. 96–161). New York: Wiley & Sons.

Perry, A. (1908). *The management of a city school.* New York: Macmillan.

Phillips, M., & Roderick, T. (2001). *The 4Rs Program: Reading, writing, respect, and resolution.* New York: Morningside Center for Teaching Social Responsibility (formerly Educators for Social Responsibility Metropolitan Area).

Pianta, R. C. (1999). *Enhancing relationships between children and teachers.* Washington, DC: American Psychological Association.

Pollock, W. (1996). *Real boys: Rescuing our sons from the myths of boyhood.* New York: Random House.

Reese, L., Vera, E., & Thompson, K. (2001, May). A qualitative investigation of perceptions of violence risk factors in low-income African American children. *Journal of Clinical Child Psychology, 30*(2), 161–171.

Rigby, K. (1996). *Bullying in schools: And what to do about it.* Melbourne: ACER.

Schonfeld, D., Kline, M., & Members of the Crisis Intervention Committee. (1994). School-based crisis intervention: An organizational model. *Crisis Intervention and Time-Limited Treatment, 1*(2), 155–166.

Schonfeld, D. J., Lichenstein, R., Kline-Pruett, M., & Speese-Linehan, D. (2002). *How to prepare for and respond to a crisis* (2nd ed.). Alexandria, VA: Association for Supervision and Curriculum Development.

Selman, R. (2003). *The Promotion of Social Awareness: Powerful Lessons from the Partnership of Developmental Theory and Classroom Practice*. New York: Russell Sage Foundation.

Selman, R. L., Beardslee, W., Schultz, L. K., Krupa, M., & Podoresky, D. (1986). Assessing adolescent interpersonal negotiation strategies: Toward the integration of structural and functional models. *Developmental Psychology, 22,* 450–459.

Shriver, T. P., Schwab-Stone, M., & DeFalco, K. (1999). Why SEL is the better way: The New Haven Social Development Program. In J. Cohen (Ed.), *Educating minds and hearts: Social emotional learning and the passage into adolescence* (pp. 43–60). New York: Teachers College Press.

Slaby, R., Wilson-Brewer, R., & Dash, K. (1994). *Aggressors, victims, and bystanders: Thinking and acting to prevent violence*. Newton, MA: Education Development Center.

Smith, P. K. (2002). *Violence in schools: The response in Europe*. London: Routledge.

Sprague, J. R., & Walker, H. M. (2000). Early identification and intervention for youth with antisocial and violent behavior. *Exceptional Children, 66,* 367–379.

Stamler, J., Cohen, J., Sandy, S., & Fisher, M. (2007). *Multi-dimensional feedback on school climate: The development and validation of the Comprehensive School Climate Inventory (CSCI)*. Submitted for publication.

Storm, M. S. (1994). *Facing history and ourselves: Holocaust and human behavior*. Boston: Facing History & Ourselves National. Available at www.facinghistory.org.

Straus, M. A., Gelles, R. J., & Steinmetz, S. K. (2006). *Violence in the American family: Behind closed doors*. New Brunswick, NJ: Transaction Publishers.

Tagiuri, T. (1968). The concept of organizational climate. In R. Tagiuri & G. H. Litevin (Eds.), *Organizational climate: Explanation of a concept*. Boston: Harvard University Press.

Twemlow, S. W. (1999). Profile of a school shooter. *Bulletin of the American Society of Psychoanalytic Physicians, 87*(2), 3–9.

Twemlow, S., Fonagy, P., & Sacco, F. C. (2002). Feeling safe in school. *Smith College Studies in Social Work, 72,* 303–326.

Twemlow, S., Fonagy, P., Sacco, F. C., Gies, M., & Hess, D. (2001). Improving the social and intellectual climate in elementary schools by addressing bully-victim-bystander relationship power struggle. In J. Cohen (Ed.), *Caring classrooms/ intelligent schools: Social emotional education of young children* (pp. 162–179). New York: Teachers College Press.

Twemlow, S. W., Fonagy, P., Sacco, F. C., & Brethour, J. R. (2006). Teachers who bully students: A hidden trauma. *International Journal of Social Psychiatry, 52*(3), 187–198.

U.S. Department of Justice. (1997). *Sex offenses and offenders*. Washington, DC: Bureau of Justice Statistics.

U.S. Department of Justice. (2000). *National trauma victimization survey*. Washington, DC: Bureau of Justice Statistics.

U.S. Secret Service. (2000). *Safe School Initiative: An interim report on the prevention of targeted violence in schools*. Washington, DC: United States Secret Service National Threat Assessment Center.

Valliant, G. E. (1977). *Adaptation to life*. Boston: Little, Brown.

Vaillant, G. (2002). *Ageing well*. Boston: Little, Brown.

Walker, H. M., Colvin, G., & Ramsey, E. (1995). *Antisocial behavior in school: Strategies and best practices*. Pacific Grove, CA: Brooks/Cole.

Watson, M., & Ecken, L. (2003). *Learning to trust: Transforming difficult elementary classrooms through developmental discipline*. San Francisco, CA: Jossey-Bass.

Weissberg, R. P., & Greenberg, M. T. (1998). School and community competence enhancement and prevention programs. In I. E. Sigel & K. A. Renninger (Eds.), *Handbook of child psychology: Vol. 4. Child psychology in practice* (5th ed., pp. 877–954). New York: John Wiley.

Weissberg, R. P., Kumpfer, K. L., & Seligman, M. E. P. (2003). Prevention that works for children and youth: An introduction. *American Psychologist, 58*(6–7), 425–432.

Whitlock, J. L. (2006). Youth perceptions of life in school: Contextual correlates of school connectedness in adolescence. *Applied Developmental Science, 10*(1), 13–29.

Willson, P., MacFarlane, J., Malecha, A., Watson, K., Lemmey, D., Schultz, P., Gist, J., & Fredland, N. (2000, September). Severity of violence against women by intimate partners and associated use of alcohol and/or illicit drugs by the perpetrator. *Journal of Interpersonal Violence, 15*(9), 996–1008.

Zigler, E., Styfco, S. J., & Gilman, E. (1993). The national Head Start program for disadvantaged preschoolers. In E. Zigler & S. J. Styfco (Eds.), *Head Start and beyond: A national plan for extended childhood intervention* (pp. 1–42). New Haven, CT: Yale University Press.

Zins, J., Weissberg, R. P., Walberg, H. W., & Wang, M. W. (Eds.). (2003). *Building school success on social and emotional learning*. New York: Teachers College Press.

Index

abuse, child, 80–84
academic achievement and safety, 4–5
adolescence, supporting of, 37
advisory periods, 74
altruistic capacities, 47–49
anger management and impulse control, 41–42
attendance and physical safety, 27–28
auto accidents, 82
avoidance behaviors, 67

body language. *See* communication skills
bullying
  altruistic capacities and, 49
  antibullying program and, 62
  at-risk students, 75
  bullies as victims, 2–3
  bystanders in, 62–63, 67–69
  defined, 64–65
  example of, 61
  impact of, 66–67
  interventions, incorporating into curriculum, 75–76
  myths about, 69–77
  parental role, 73
  prevalence of, 65–66
  role plays for, 74–75
  school shootings and, 62–63
  scripts to prevent, 23, 73–75
  by teachers, 66
  trauma and, 83

as triadic relationship, 67–69, 71
upstanders, reinforcement of, 76–77
bystanders, 62–63, 67–69

car accidents, 82
Center for Social and Emotional Education, 50, 73–74, 110
character education. *See* social emotional learning
child abuse, 80–84
classroom rules, 57–58
Columbine High School, 4, 62
communication skills, 33–37, 39–41
community service and service learning, 51
Comprehensive School Climate Inventory, 99
cooperative capacities, 42–44
core competencies
  altruistic capacities, 47–49
  communication capacities, 39–41
  cooperative capacities, 42–44
  diversity appreciation, 45–47
  friendship formation, 44–45
  impulse control and anger management, 41–42
  problem-solving and decision-making, 37–39
  reflective and empathic abilities, 33–37
  summary of, 52–53

About the Authors and Contributors

John Devine is an urban anthropologist who has studied and worked in inner-city schools for many years. At New York University, he founded and directed the highly successful School Partnership Program, a tutoring, mentoring, and research initiative that operated in several New York City public schools. His ethnographic research attempts to identify political and ideological patterns underlying structural violence and to investigate institutional responses for preventing violence. He is the author of an award-winning ethnography, *Maximum Security: The Culture of Violence in Inner-City Schools* (University of Chicago Press, 1996) and numerous articles and papers dealing with social and emotional issues in school settings.

After the tragic events at Columbine High School, President Clinton appointed him as the chair of the Academic Advisory Council of the National Campaign Against Youth Violence. He was a founding member of the international coalition that organized the First International Conference on School Violence Prevention in Paris in March 2001. He is currently a faculty member and director of the School Safety Program at the Center for Social and Emotional Education, a nonprofit organization dedicated to inculcating social and emotional competencies (www.csee.net) in schools and communities.

A former Jesuit priest and a former member of the theology faculty at Georgetown University, he holds graduate degrees in theology, anthropology, and international education. He is married to Frances Elizabeth Duffee Devine. They are blessed with five children and seven grandchildren.

Jonathan Cohen is a clinical psychologist and educator. He has worked with children, families, and K–12 schools for over 30 years in a variety of roles: special education teacher, school psychologist, program developer, consultant, psychoeducational diagnostician, child and adult clinical psychologist, and psychoanalyst.

Jonathan is the cofounder and president of the Center for Social and Emotional Education (www.csee.net). He is also an Adjunct Professor in Psychology and Education, Teachers College, Columbia University, and Adjunct Professor in Education, School of Professional Studies, City University of New York.

He is the author of over 60 papers and books including, the award-winning *Educating Minds and Hearts* (Teachers College Press, 1999) and *Caring Classrooms/Intelligent Schools* (Teachers College Press, 2001). He lectures and consults nationally and internationally. He is married and the proud father of two children.

Roy Lubit is a child, adolescent, adult, and forensic psychiatrist. He has consulted extensively to schools in Manhattan and to mental health professionals in America, Europe, and the Middle East on helping children in stressful conditions. He is a member of the Consortium for the Study of Emotional Intelligence in Organizations and of the Center for Emotional Intelligence in Organizations.

David J. Schonfeld is a developmental-behavioral pediatrician and the Thelma and Jack Rubinstein Professor of Pediatrics, Director of the Division of Developmental and Behavioral Pediatrics, and Director of the National Center for School Crisis and Bereavement at Cincinnati Children's Hospital Medical Center. He has authored articles, book chapters, and a handbook (published by ASCD) on school crisis preparedness.